THIS BOOK IS A GIFT TO:

_____

FROM:

_____

DATE:

_____

Walking with the Savior

Copyright © 1993 by Max Lucado.
Quotations from Max Lucado compiled by Karen Hill.
Originally published as an inspirational calendar
under the title *Walking with the Savior* by Max Lucado.

Published by Christian Art Publishers
PO Box 1599, Vereeniging, 1930, RSA

© 2017
First edition 2017

Designed by Christian Art Publishers

Images used under license from Shutterstock.com

Scripture quotations are taken from the *Holy Bible*, New Century Version®.
Copyright © 1987, 1988, 1991, 2005 by Word Publishing, a division of Thomas
Nelson, Inc. Used by permission.

Printed in China

ISBN 978-1-4321-1623-1

18 19 20 21 22 23 24 25 26 27 – 13 12 11 10 9 8 7 6 5 4

Walking

WITH THE

Savior

MAX LUCADO

CHRISTIAN ART PUBLISHERS

INTRODUCTION

Walking with the Savior will take you on an inspired faith walk with Christ as you seek Him day by day.

In this yearlong devotional, selected insightful writings from Max Lucado combine with a favorite passage from Scripture to guide your steps and restore your faith.

The thoughtful bite-sized devotions will enlighten your path as you take time to pause and breathe in God's Word.

January

January 1

CITIZENSHIP IN HEAVEN

"I tell you the truth,
whoever hears what I say
and believes in the One who
sent Me has eternal life."

John 5:24

With the coming of another year we are reminded that time is passing. The grains of sand are dripping through the hourglass; sometimes they seem to pass so quickly. That is a frightening thing for those who have no hope. But for those of us whose citizenship is in heaven, it's only good and it's only right.

January 2

PEACE IN ME

"I told you these things so that you can have peace in Me. In this world you will have trouble, but be brave! I have defeated the world."

John 16:33

Could you use some peace in your life today? When your life is in turmoil and you wonder if there will ever be another peaceful day for you, open your heart to the God of peace and to Jesus, the Prince of Peace. They will envelop you in a peace that transcends understanding.

January 3

DWELLING IN THE HIGHLANDS

Jesus has the power of God, by which He has
given us everything we need to live and to serve God.
We have these things because we know Him.
Jesus called us by His glory and goodness.

2 Peter 1:3

Jesus has come into our dark hearts
and extended a hand – He has
broken in from the outside by an act of
God and has lifted us back up. Spiritually,
we are secure. We're dwelling in the high-
lands with Him.

January 4

LIFTED UP BY HIS MERCY

So I bow in prayer before the Father from whom
every family in heaven and on earth gets its true name.
I ask the Father in His great glory to give you the
power to be strong inwardly through His Spirit.
I pray that Christ will live in your hearts by faith and
that your life will be strong in love and be built on love.

Ephesians 3:14–17

Prayer is the recognition that if God had not engaged Himself in our problems, we would still be lost in the blackness. It is by His mercy that we have been lifted up. Prayer is that whole process that reminds us of who God is and who we are.

January 5

FORGIVENESS

I pray that you and all God's holy people
will have the power to understand the greatness
of Christ's love - how wide and how long and
how high and how deep that love is.

Ephesians 3:18

When you forgive someone, you are as close to God as you will ever be, because in that forgiveness you are demonstrating the very heart of God, the merciful King. If you want to understand God, if you want to draw closer to Him, then forgive someone today.

SOURCE OF LIGHT
AND STRENGTH

Since you were a child you have known the Holy
Scriptures which are able to make you wise. And that
wisdom leads to salvation through faith in Christ Jesus.

2 Timothy 3:15

*F*ather, make us aware of how precious Your Word is. Bless those
who transport Your Word to far-off places,
to people who haven't been able to open
Your Word. Thank You, Father, for giving
us this source of light and strength, and
for giving us the opportunity to uncover
the jewels waiting to be discovered in
Your holy pages.

January 7

GIFTS OF LOVE

LORD All-Powerful, happy are
the people who trust You!

Psalm 84:12

Father, You have expressed toward us unlimited mercy. The only reason this world continues is because You have mercy upon us. Millions of people today are receiving food for which they'll never give thanks. We're breathing air that we take for granted. Somehow, though, You continue to feed us with Your mercy and forgiveness. Thank You for the unimaginable gifts of Your love.

January 8

EQUIPPING YOU

He gives strength to those who are tired and more
power to those who are weak ... But the people
who trust the LORD will become strong again. They
will rise up as an eagle in the sky; they will run and
not need rest; they will walk and not become tired.

Isaiah 40:29, 31

You get impatient with your own life, trying to master a habit or control a sin and in your frustration begin to wonder where the power of God is. Be patient. God is using today's difficulties to strengthen you for tomorrow. He is *equipping* you. The God who makes things grow will help you bear fruit.

January 9

HUMILITY

The LORD is pleased with His people;
He saves the humble.

Psalm 149:4

God exalts humility. When God works in our lives, helping us to become humble, He gives us a permanent joy: humility gives us a joy that cannot be taken away.

January 10

THE FOUNDATION

You have not seen Christ, but still you love Him.
You cannot see Him now, but you believe in Him.
So you are filled with a joy that cannot
be explained, a joy full of glory.

1 Peter 1:8

I believe that a carpenter, the Nazarene carpenter with the Galilean accent and calloused hands, was not merely a man, but He was God. That's the foundation upon which you must build. It's the foundation that says, "My sins have been taken care of, my life has a purpose, and death holds no power over me because I believe in the death conqueror."

January 11

THOSE HANDS

"I leave you peace; My peace I give you ...
So don't let your hearts be troubled or afraid."

John 14:27

We serve the God who designed the universe and set our world in motion. But those hands that hung the stars in the heavens also wiped away the tears of the widow and the leper. And they will wipe away your tears as well.

January 12

HE SIMPLY WAITS

The Lord is not slow in doing what He promised –
the way some people understand slowness.
But God is being patient with you. He does not want
anyone to be lost, but He wants all people
to change their hearts and lives.

2 Peter 3:9

It's God's greatest dream for you to go to heaven – His priority is to get you into His kingdom. And yet, though He is sovereign, He never forces His will on any human being – He simply waits on your acknowledgment of Him as Lord.

January 13

GUARD YOUR HEART!

Do not give the devil
a way to defeat you.

Ephesians 4:27

I am terribly concerned as I hear more and more about how people flirt with immorality and how people dance with materialism and how they consider themselves invulnerable to Satan. We are not invulnerable to Satan – he's wise, he's crafty ... and just as God wishes you to spend forever with Him in heaven, Satan wishes you to spend eternity separated from God. Guard your heart!

January 14

MY HELP COMES FROM THE LORD

I look up to the hills, but where does my help come from? My help comes from the LORD, who made heaven and earth.

Psalm 121:1-2

Are you discouraged? Are you weary? You've been promised a life of rest. You've been promised eternity. Even in the face of death we should not grow discouraged, but we do. Let your prayer be that God will empower His Word with His Spirit to blow away the clouds of discouragement circling overhead and increase your courage and faith.

January 15

ONE DAY AT A TIME

God, my strength, I will sing praises to You.
God, my defender, You are the God who loves me.

Psalm 59:17

Life is too big to be resolved in one day ... just take the challenges that come your way one day at a time.

January 16

GOD'S GRACE

I trust in Your love.
My heart is happy because You saved me.
I sing to the LORD because
He has taken care of me.

Psalm 13:5-6

*T*he gospels are like a tapestry, woven together with two incredible points: the immeasurable value of each person and the unimaginable depth of God's grace.

TO CATCH A GLIMPSE

As you received Christ Jesus the Lord,
so continue to live in Him.
Keep your roots deep in Him
and have your lives built on Him.

Colossians 2:6-7

In essence, Christianity is nothing more, nothing less than a desire and an effort to see Jesus. That's all it is. We're trying to catch a glimpse of a man, not a program, not a plan, not a system, not a doctrine. We're trying to see a man who called Himself the Son of God.

January 18

YOU FORMED ME

You made my whole being; You formed me in my mother's body. I praise You because You made me in an amazing and wonderful way. What You have done is wonderful. I know this very well.

Psalm 139:13-14

When you wake up and look in the mirror in the morning, you're seeing God's *poetry*. You may think He's not much of a poet, but when God wove you together, it was not by accident, it was not happenstance, it was not a mistake. You are the result of all the creative energy of an omnipotent, omnipresent, and omniscient God poured into the formation of humanity.

January 19

GOD LOVES ME

My God loves me, and He goes in front of me.
He will help me defeat my enemies.

Psalm 59:10

Over and over Jesus would do the same thing and tell the same story: He would love Nicodemus, so caught up in false religion, but would hate the false religion; He would love the woman caught in adultery, but condemn the adultery; He would love Zaccheus, so obsessed by his possessions, but hate his materialism. He would love the sinner, but hate the sin.

January 20

NOTHING BESIDES YOU

I have no one in heaven but You;
I want nothing on earth besides You.

Psalm 73:25

*T*he love of Christ compels us to do
what we never thought we could
do and go to heights we never thought
we could reach. Precious is the name of
Jesus!

January 21

GOD MEETS OUR NEEDS

Don't say, "I'll pay you back for the wrong you did."
Wait for the LORD, and He will make things right.

Proverbs 20:22

*S*ometimes life doesn't seem fair, does it? Have you ever wondered why good people have to hurt? Why the innocent suffer? Often it seems that those who have been most battered by life seem to understand Jesus best, and His assurance finds its way into the darkest corners of life because, regardless of our circumstances, God meets our needs. By surrendering to Him, the ultimate victory is ours.

January 22

TRULY FREE!

But I will sing about Your strength.
In the morning I will sing about Your love.
You are my defender, my place of
safety in times of trouble.

Psalm 59:16

We have been liberated from our own guilt and our own legalism. We have the freedom to pray and the freedom to love the God of our hearts. And we have been forgiven by the only one who could condemn us. We are truly free!

January 23

FORGIVE EACH OTHER

Be kind and loving to each other,
and forgive each other
just as God forgave you in Christ.

Ephesians 4:32

*O*ur forgiveness of others is a signal
of our awareness of how much
God has given us.

January 24

ETERNAL TREASURES

"Don't store treasures for yourselves here on
earth ... But store your treasures in heaven
where they cannot be destroyed by moths or rust
and where thieves cannot break in and steal them.
Your heart will be where your treasure is."

Matthew 6:19-21

*F*ather, keep us from being so
blinded by possessions that we
cannot keep that we would fail to see the
eternal treasure we cannot lose.

January 25

BEFORE GOD'S THRONE

Let us, then, feel very sure that we can come before God's throne where there is grace. There we can receive mercy and grace to help us when we need it.

Hebrews 4:16

In our "bootstrap" society, where you tough it up and do it on your own and take pride in being a rugged individualist, the one thing that seems to escape us is being before God on our knees, being before God aware that we are helpless, and *allowing* Him to assist us.

January 26

ALL THIS IS FROM GOD

All this is from God. Through Christ,
God made peace between us and Himself,
and God gave us the work of telling everyone
about the peace we can have with Him.

2 Corinthians 5:18

*B*lessed Lord and God, we come to You, aware that You have pierced our world. You became flesh, You dwelled among us, You saw us in our fallen state, You reached in and pulled us out. You offered us salvation, You offered us mercy. And we are ever thankful.

January 27

REMIND US

I want to know Christ and the power that raised Him from the dead. I want to share in His sufferings and become like Him in His death. Then I have hope that I myself will be raised from the dead.

Philippians 3:10-11

*L*et us ask our Father humbly, yet confidently in the name of Jesus, to remind us of the empty tomb. Let us see the victorious Jesus: the conqueror of the tomb, the one who defied death. And let us be reminded that we, too, will be granted that same victory!

January 28

PRAISE THE LORD

Praise the LORD for the glory of His name;
worship the LORD because He is holy.

Psalm 29:2

*P*raise is the highest occupation of any being. What happens when we praise the Father? We re-establish the proper chain of command; we recognize that the King is on the throne and that He has saved His people.

January 29

HIS GIFT OF MERCY

I mean that you have been saved by grace
through believing. You did not save yourselves;
it was a gift from God.

Ephesians 2:8

God forgave us before we even asked
it. He extended mercy to us before we
even knew we needed it. Why? Because
the God of mercy took pity on us — a band
of creatures who are incapable of saving
themselves without His gift of mercy.

January 30

CRY OUT FOR WISDOM

Listen carefully to wisdom; set your mind on understanding. Cry out for wisdom, and beg for understanding. Search for it like silver, and hunt for it like hidden treasure. Then you will understand respect for the LORD, and you will find that you know God.

Proverbs 2:2-5

Do you have a hunger for the Word of God? I challenge you to rediscover the Bible in your own life ... to regain the same hunger and enthusiasm you felt when you first heard the name of Jesus!

January 31

THE RIVER OF ETERNITY

This is what God told us: God has given
us eternal life, and this life is in His Son.

1 John 5:11

*S*everal hundred years before Jesus,
Isaiah said that there is one who
is chosen; there is one who is promised.
He said that something would happen that
would convince us that we're not spinning
in a whirlpool headed toward nowhere, but
we're floating down the river of eternity
guided by God.

February

February 1

LIVE IN PEACE

Wish good for those who harm you;
wish them well and do not curse them. Be happy
with those who are happy, and be sad with those
who are sad. Live in peace with each other.

Romans 12:14-16

Who are peacemakers? They are the first ones who take the initiative and *decide* to extend their hands as olive branches of peace. If someone has hurt you, it is *your* responsibility to rebuild the bridge of relationship.

February 2

JUST AS WE ARE

Now may God Himself, the God of peace, make you pure, belonging only to Him. May your whole self — spirit, soul, and body — be kept safe and without fault when our LORD Jesus Christ comes.

1 Thessalonians 5:23

*H*ere we are, Father. We call ourselves Your people, yet we carry the baggage of a week of concerns. We come to You just as we are, without trying to hide our mistakes. Father, mend us and make us better than we could be alone. Take that which is broken in our lives and make it stronger at the broken places. And use that new strength in Your kingdom.

February 3

BE PATIENT

Depend on the LORD; trust Him,
and He will take care of you.

Psalm 37:5

Don't hurry God. The problems that we think may drown us today could be the very stepping-stones to greater spiritual strength tomorrow. Throughout Scripture we are reminded to be patient in suffering, in physical distress, in emotional discouragement. The Father will supply your needs. Don't hurry God.

February 4

PERFECT COMMUNION

In Christ we can come before God
with freedom and without fear.
We can do this through faith in Christ.

Ephesians 3:12

*P*rayer is the most powerful tool in God's kingdom, because in prayer we are in perfect communion with God, interceding with the Father on behalf of His creation. The majesty of prayer puts us in the relationship God intended to have with man: perfect communion.

February 5

BUILDING BRIDGES

It is good and pleasant when
God's people live together in peace!

Psalm 133:1

*G*od of peace, Father of comfort, we
pray that Your kingdom would come
into our hearts and that peace would rule.
Teach us what it means to be peacemakers. Help us cultivate peace between
others and You in our neighborhoods,
offices, school rooms. Teach us the art of
building bridges and not walls. We glorify
Your name, the great God of peace.

February 6

SHOW MERCY

"Love your enemies. Do good to those
who hate you, bless those who curse you,
pray for those who are cruel to you ...
Show mercy, just as your Father shows mercy."

Luke 6:27-28, 36

What do you do when people mistreat you or those you love? Does the fire of anger boil within you, with leaping flames consuming your emotions? Or do you reach somewhere, to some source of cool water and pull out a bucket of mercy — to free yourself? Is there any emotion that imprisons the soul more than the unwillingness to forgive? Can you reach for that cool water of forgiveness today?

February 7

GOD'S TEACHING

But the truly happy people are those who carefully study God's perfect law that makes people free, and they continue to study it. They do not forget what they heard, but they obey what God's teaching says. Those who do this will be made happy.

James 1:25

If you want to grow in the Word of God, become a person with a chisel and quarry the Word — look, explore, seek. Let the Word become your Word, and you will grow.

THOSE WHO FOLLOW CHRIST

Then people will say, "There really are
rewards for doing what is right.
There really is a God who judges the world."

Psalm 58:11

Listen to the Christ rather than to the voices of men. Jesus says you can't please men and still be a servant of God. Those who listen and follow Christ will be received into heaven by the pierced hands of the One who knows the freedom of giving up what you cannot own in order to receive what no one can take from you — eternal life.

February 9

SUCH A PRIVILEGE

Yes, it is through Christ
we all have the right to come
to the Father in one Spirit.

Ephesians 2:18

*F*ather, it's with earnestness that we come to You, asking You to open our hearts and let the drafts of heaven come inside. Thank You for the great blessing You've given us in allowing us to come to You in prayer and stand in Your presence. Holy is Your name that You would allow us to have such a privilege.

AN UNQUENCHABLE BELIEF

This is how God showed His love to us:
He sent His one and only Son into the
world so that we could have life through Him.

1 John 4:9

The fire that lit the boiler of the New Testament church was an unquenchable belief that if Jesus had been only a man, He would have stayed in the tomb. They couldn't stay silent about the fact that the One they saw hung on a cross, walked again on the earth and appeared to 500 people. I wonder if sometimes we stay silent because we've forgotten the One who was on that cross.

February 11

REGATHER STRENGTH

God rested from all His works.

Hebrews 4:4

*S*ometimes the most godly thing we can do for ourselves is to go to sleep. Sometimes the most godly thing we can do for our family and friends is to take a break and regather our strength.

February 12

REMEMBER THE LORD

"I will be with you always,
even until the end of this age."

Matthew 28:20

Remember the Lord. Remember who is in control. Remember His goodness in the past. Remember God's closeness in the present. Remember His power for the future.

February 13

RESIST DISCOURAGEMENT

The sun cannot hurt you during the day, and the
moon cannot hurt you at night. The LORD will protect
you from all dangers; He will guard your life.

Psalm 121:6-7

*R*esist discouragement. Don't let
it control you. Nobody can take
away from you your capacity to make a
decision regarding discouragement. You
have the power to determine not to let
discouraging circumstances engulf you.
As Christians who can call on the power
of God, we have every reason not to
feel discouraged.

February 14

HIS VERY BEST!

This is what real love is:
It is not our love for God;
it is God's love for us.
He sent His Son to die in our place
to take away our sins.

1 John 4:10

I hope you receive a rose or a special card from that special person today. If you didn't and don't expect to, remember that the One who loves you most has already sent you His very best!

February 15

BRING YOUR FEARS TO ME

Don't be afraid of what they fear;
do not dread those things.

1 Peter 3:14

Jesus is not afraid of the things that cause us fear. He never said, "Don't bring your fears to Me; I'm too busy." Instead, He said, "I'm not afraid of the things that cause you fear. Bring your fears to Me."

February 16

LISTENING TO
THE WRONG VOICE

My dear friends, many false prophets have gone out
into the world. So do not believe every spirit, but
test the spirits to see if they are from God.

1 John 4:1

*H*ave you ever listened to the
wrong voice? Have you ever
taken the wrong advice? Oftentimes the
cause of a crisis in our lives is that we
listen to the wrong voice. To whose voice
will you listen today?

February 17

BUILD ONLY ON FAITH

The people who obey God's commands live in God,
and God lives in them. We know that God lives
in us because of the Spirit God gave us.

1 John 3:24

Don't build your house on a career. Don't build your house on a thrill. Don't build your house on a talent. Don't build your house on one solitary earthly relationship. Don't pursue things that don't last. Build your house on the only thing that can last: faith.

February 18

A NEW DAY

With the loving mercy of our God,
a new day from heaven will dawn upon us.

Luke 1:78

Perhaps the heaviest burden we try to carry is the burden of mistakes, failures. What do you do with your failures? Do you carry them around with you? We can't carry our mistakes alone – somebody has to help us carry them. God doesn't want you burdened with past failures. He wants you freed of them, and He's the only One who can give you that freedom.

February 19

THE SOURCE OF STRENGTH

Strengthen yourselves so that you will
live here on earth doing what God wants,
not the evil things people want.

1 Peter 4:2

*T*he most powerful life is the most
simple life. The most powerful life
is the life that knows where it's going,
that knows where the source of strength
is, and the life that stays free of clutter
and happenstance and hurriedness.

February 20

LOVE AND TRUTH

Love and truth belong to God's people;
goodness and peace will be theirs.

Psalm 85:10

*P*eace is never sought at the expense of truth. God never calls
us into a relationship with Him just to
have a relationship. He sets truth in front
of us and says, "Agree to that truth and
then we can have a relationship."

February 21

MAKE PRAYER A PRIORITY

Continue praying, keeping alert,
and always thanking God.

Colossians 4:2

ather, when You were on earth, You prayed. You prayed in the morning, You prayed at night, You prayed alone, You prayed with people. In Your hours of distress You retreated into times of prayer. In Your hours of joy You lifted Your heart and hands to the Father in prayer. Help us to be more like You in this way ... help us to make prayer a priority in our daily lives.

February 22

GOD IS MERCIFUL

God, be merciful to me because You are loving.
Because You are always ready to be merciful,
wipe out all my wrongs.

Psalm 51:1

We have nothing to offer God in exchange for what He has given us. It's not that we don't have any value; it's just that we don't have any right to request the forgiveness we so desperately need and which He is so willing to share.

February 23

TOTAL SURRENDER

But if we confess our sins, He will forgive our sins,
because we can trust God to do what is right.
He will cleanse us from all the wrongs we have done.

1 John 1:9

We don't like to recognize our ruin, but that's where Jesus begins. Once we're honest with ourselves about who we are, then God can begin to remold our hearts ... total surrender.

February 24

THE WORDS PIERCE

God's word is alive and working and is sharper
than a double-edged sword. It cuts all the way
into us, where the soul and the spirit are joined,
to the center of our joints and bones. And it
judges the thoughts and feelings in our hearts.

Hebrews 4:12

We go to the Word of God for comfort, and when we do, the words pierce like a surgeon's scalpel, both cutting and healing. The Word of God cuts to the very place where thoughts and attitudes come together, at the juncture of soul and spirit, providing a healing that can be obtained in no other way on earth.

February 25

CALL TO HIM

I love the LORD, because He listens to
my prayers for help. He paid attention to me,
so I will call to Him for help as long as I live.

Psalm 116:1-2

God is an exalted Friend, a holy
Father, and an elevated King. How
do we approach Him – as King, as Father,
or as Friend? The answer: yes!

February 26

GET RID OF THE RUBBLE

The LORD defends those who suffer;
He defends them in times of trouble.

Psalm 9:9

Does the rubble of your life take you off course and cause frustration? Get rid of the rubble – organize your day, decide where to start and where to finish. Sometimes we think that being a Christian means saying yes to every request that comes our way. Sometimes you are being more faithful by being disciplined and knowing where to use your gifts. Put your strengths on strengths.

February 27

IF ONLY WE'LL WAIT

The LORD does what is right, and He loves justice,
so honest people will see His face.

Psalm 11:7

*F*ather, nothing is louder than the silence of our God. But Father, forgive us for the times we've interpreted Your silence as a lack of love. Give us patience, for we know You'll answer, Father, if only we'll wait.

February 28

SET ON THE COURSE

Trust the LORD with all your heart,
and don't depend on your own understanding.
Remember the LORD in all you do,
and He will give you success.

Proverbs 3:5-6

We know that someday our heavenly Father is going to take all those who follow Him into eternal happiness. It's to that day that we look. It's upon our hope and confidence that He will return that we stand. Our prayer should be that our Father will help us make decisions that will set us on the course of eternal life.

February 29

IT'S NOT FAIR

Those who are honest will live in the land,
and those who are innocent will remain in it.
But the wicked will be removed from the land,
and the unfaithful will be thrown out of it.

Proverbs 2:21-22

When we look at the world around us, sometimes it's difficult to understand the unfairness of life. It's not fair that the young should suffer. It's not fair that the innocent should go hungry. But nor is it fair that a God would have to come to earth and hang on His own cross to protect us from the evil one. It's not fair ... but that's *love*. And that's God.

March

March 1

PEOPLE OF GOD

This service you do not only helps the needs of God's people, it also brings many more thanks to God. It is a proof of our faith. Many people will praise God because you obey the Good News of Christ - the gospel you say you believe - and because you freely share with them and with all others.

2 Corinthians 9:12-13

*T*here is a special place in our hearts for people who have names we cannot even pronounce and speak languages we cannot speak, and live in places we'll never visit who are, as we are, people of God.

March 2

THE TRUE GRACE

This is the true grace of God.
Stand strong in that grace.

1 Peter 5:12

We're not perfect, Father, but we are Yours. We're not what we should be, but we do claim Your salvation and Your grace. We ask You to make us every day more and more into the image of Jesus Christ. We stand amazed that You would have such mercy upon us to forgive us time and time again. Thank You for the immeasurable depth of Your grace.

March 3

A SEED OF PEACE

"I am the LORD your God, who teaches you to do what is good, who leads you in the way you should go. If you had obeyed Me, you would have had peace like a full-flowing river."

Isaiah 48:17-18

Perhaps the seeds you sow in your areas of conflict won't reach maturity tomorrow, next week or even for a generation. Does that mean you shouldn't sow the seeds *immediately*? Never underestimate the power of a seed of peace: the power of a kind word, a seed of apology, a phone call, an explanation. This is the way we serve a God of peace.

March 4

WHEN GOD'S
PEOPLE INTERCEDE

When a believing person prays,
great things happen.

James 5:16

*G*od's power is unleashed when
God's people intercede.

March 5

THOSE WHO
WIN THE VICTORY

"Those who win the victory will sit with Me on
My throne in the same way that I won the victory
and sat down with My Father on His throne."

Revelation 3:21

believe that praise and prayer
develop us for what we will do
when we arrive in heaven. What's your
picture of what you'll be doing there –
sitting on a cloud? Polishing your halo?
Playing your harp? That's not what
you're going to be doing. You're going
to be involved in the ongoing process
of co-reigning with God.

March 6

POSSIBLE TO FORGIVE

"Don't judge others, and you will not be judged.
Don't accuse others of being guilty,
and you will not be accused of being guilty.
Forgive, and you will be forgiven."

Luke 6:37

*G*o back to the Cross and see how God through the Cross forgives us: that gives us strength to forgive each other. We have a mandate to forgive, a liberating concept that says you have a choice. You don't have to live with anger or resentment – you can get rid of it. It *is* possible to forgive – through prayer and the Holy Spirit, it is possible!

March 7

THE TEACHING OF CHRIST

Let the teaching of Christ live in you richly.
Use all wisdom to teach and instruct each
other by singing psalms, hymns, and spiritual
songs with thankfulness in your hearts to God.

Colossians 3:16

*T*he purpose of the Christian life is not to memorize the Bible just for the sake of memorizing the text. The Bible was provided for us as a vehicle to carry us so that we might be able to see Jesus Christ.

THY KINGDOM COME

So that every knee will bow to the
name of Jesus – everyone in heaven, on earth,
and under the earth. And everyone will confess that
Jesus Christ is Lord and bring glory to God the Father.

Philippians 2:10-11

Thy kingdom come, Lord. Let Your kingdom live in the hearts of people, let Your kingdom live in society, let the church be strong, and let Your kingdom come eternally.

March 9

WORTHY OF PRAISE

I will praise the LORD at all times;
His praise is always on my lips.
My whole being praises the LORD.

Psalm 34:1-2

We should serve God even if there is darkness enveloping our lives and even if we don't understand what's happening ... even when the circumstances of our lives don't make sense: Because He is worthy of praise, *because He is God*.

March 10

DEEP GRACE

Where can I go to get away from Your Spirit?
Where can I run from You?
If I go up to the heavens, You are there.
If I lie down in the grave, You are there.

Psalm 139:7-8

Always remember that Jesus says, "My grace is deeper than your sins."

March 11

HIS LOST SHEEP

Anyone who brings a sinner back
from the wrong way will save
that sinner's soul from death and
will cause many sins to be forgiven.

James 5:20

I wonder if Jesus doesn't muster up a slight smile as He sees His lost sheep come straggling into the fold – the beaten, broken, dirty sheep who stands at the door looking up at the Shepherd asking, "Can I come in? I don't deserve it, but is there room in Your kingdom for one more?" The Shepherd looks down at the sheep and says, "Come in, this is your home."

THE ONE CALLED JESUS

Those who preached the Good News
to you told you those things with the help of
the Holy Spirit who was sent from heaven –
things into which angels desire to look.

1 Peter 1:12

Of all the unusual beginnings, there is none more unusual than that of Christianity. The church of our Lord was begun by a group of reluctant followers in a second-story room in Jerusalem. They were timid followers, hesitant soldiers, speechless messengers. They didn't know what to do; they didn't know what to say; but they knew they could not forget the one called Jesus.

eMarch 13

GOD'S COMPASS

"Make them ready for Your service through
Your truth; Your teaching is truth."

John 17:17

Just as a navigator can't find his
destination without a compass, we
can't find peace without God's compass –
the Word of Truth.

THE MINISTRY OF PRAYER

Pray continually, and give thanks whatever happens.
That is what God wants for you in Christ Jesus.

1 Thessalonians 5:17-18

We should be people of great prayer. We should be prayer warriors. We should be people who use the ministry of prayer to its fullest capacity. The highest and greatest calling of Christians is the ministry of prayer.

March 15

GREAT MERCY

God's mercy is great, and He loved us very much.
Though we were spiritually dead because of the
things we did against God, He gave us new life with
Christ. You have been saved by God's grace.

Ephesians 2:4-5

The first step toward forgiveness is to see the other person as a human being, not as a source of hurt. That's how God treated us with mercy – He became one of us, He felt as we feel, He understood our frustrations. And as a result, when He hung on the cross, He could look at those crucifying Him and ask God to forgive them.

THE RIGHT FOUNDATION

"They are blessed who hunger and thirst
after justice, for they will be satisfied."

Matthew 5:6

*T*he Beatitudes are not suggestions, good ideas, theories for a positive mental attitude – they are the rules for right living. Those that hear them and obey them are building on the right foundation.

March 17

DO YOU WORRY?

All living things look to You for food,
and You give it to them at the right time.
You open Your hand, and You satisfy all living things.

Psalm 145:15-16

The word *worry* comes from a word that means "to divide." When you worry, you divide your energy. Do you worry? I worry about you if you don't worry! All of us worry, but we shouldn't. Jesus commands us half a dozen times, "Do not worry." When we worry about a situation, the problem gets us instead of us getting it.

March 18

TO THE LAMB BE PRAISE

Then I heard all creatures in heaven and on earth and
under the earth and in the sea saying: "To the One
who sits on the throne and to the Lamb be praise
and honor and glory and power forever and ever."

Revelation 5:13

The whole purpose of coming before
the King is to praise Him, to live
in recognition of His splendor. Praise –
lifting up our hearts and hands, exulting
with our voices, singing His praises – is
the occupation of those who dwell in the
kingdom.

March 19

TRUST IN THE LORD

God, I look to You for help. I trust in You, Lord.

Psalm 141:8

Don't put your hope in things that can change – relationships, money, talents, beauty, even health. Set your sights on the one thing that can never change: trust in your heavenly Father.

eMarch 20

SHARING GOD'S GLORY

Since we have been made right with God by our faith, we have peace with God. This happened through our Lord Jesus Christ, who has brought us into that blessing of God's grace that we now enjoy. And we are happy because of the hope we have of sharing God's glory.

Romans 5:1-2

When we look at the cross, we feel only gratitude. We thank You, Father, that on the cross You provided forgiveness for our sins, purpose for our lives, and an answer for our death. We believe that the tomb couldn't hold You in and that death couldn't keep You down. We believe that when we speak to You, Father, we are addressing the death conqueror.

FOLLOW THE TEACHINGS

Everything that was written in the past
was written to teach us.
The Scriptures give us patience and
encouragement so that we can have hope.

Romans 15:4

Your life came with an owner's man-
ual – if you follow the teachings in
it, you will be fully equipped and your life
will operate much more smoothly.

March 22

FULLY UNITED IN PRAYER

"When you are praying, if you are angry
with someone, forgive him so that your
Father in heaven will also forgive your sins."

Mark 11:25

Isn't it presumptuous to come to the throne of grace if we haven't been gracious to the people in our lives? How can we approach a God of mercy if we ourselves have hearts full of bitterness or anger? We must take care of relationship problems – make up with a spouse, get along with fellow church members, love our neighbors – then we will be fully united in prayer with the Father.

March 23

RECOGNIZE YOUR PRIZE

I pray also that you will have greater
understanding in your heart so you will know
the hope to which He has called us and
that you will know how rich and glorious are
the blessings God has promised His holy people.

Ephesians 1:18

Jesus says the way to deal with
your problems is to recognize your
prize. You see, if we have a prize that's
great enough, our problems become small.
There will be problems on this earth, but
there will be a place where you'll be
saved if you'll endure.

March 24

ASSURED OF VICTORY

Live such good lives that they will see the good things you do and will give glory to God on the day when Christ comes again.

1 Peter 2:12

If you have no faith in the future, then you have no power in the present. If you have no faith in the life beyond this life, then your present life is going to be powerless. But if you believe in the future and are assured of victory, then there should be a dance in your step and a smile on your face.

March 25

PRAY IN THE SPIRIT

Pray in the Spirit at all times with all kinds
of prayers, asking for everything you need.
To do this you must always be ready and never
give up. Always pray for all God's people.

Ephesians 6:18

would like to encourage you, ad-
monish you to make a decision to
pray more and to set up some specific
plans to support that decision. Will you
determine in your heart to pray more?
Will you start a prayer group in your
home? Pray continually – live in a spirit
of prayer.

A SAVIOR WHO CAME DOWN

For this reason Jesus had to be made like
His brothers in every way so He could be their
merciful and faithful high priest in service to God.

Hebrews 2:17

Our God is not aloof – He's not so far above us that He can't see and understand our problems. Jesus isn't a God who stayed on the mountaintop – He's a Savior who came down and lived and worked with the people. Everywhere He went, the crowds followed, drawn together by the magnet that was – and is – the Savior.

March 27

GOD'S TENDERNESS

He takes care of His people like a shepherd.
He gathers them like lambs in His arms
and carries them close to Him.

Isaiah 40:11

*W*e have been touched by God's tenderness – all the tenderness of a gentle father. He doesn't come quarrelling and wrangling and forcing His way into anyone's heart. He comes into our hearts like a gentle lamb, not a roaring lion.

March 28

YOU HAVE WON!

The LORD is not slow in doing what He promised -
the way some people understand slowness.
But God is being patient with you. He does
not want anyone to be lost, but He wants
all people to change their hearts and lives.

2 Peter 3:9

What is unique about the king-dom of God is that you are assured of victory. You have won! You are assured that you will someday stand before the face of God and see the King of kings. You are assured that someday you will enter a world where there will be no more pain, no more tears, no more sorrow.

March 29

PEACEMAKERS

"They are blessed who work for peace,
for they will be called God's children."

Matthew 5:9

Make us, O God, into Your peacemakers. Give us courage as we stand on fields of daily conflict. Let us be tools of reconciliation; let us be ambassadors of love; let us be as You are – peacemakers, that we may be called sons of God.

March 30

YOU KNOW EVERYTHING

You know when I sit down and when I get up.
You know my thoughts before I think them.
You know where I go and where I lie down.
You know everything I do.

Psalm 139:2-3

Perhaps the reason that God doesn't always give us the answer to the *whys* of our existence is that He knows we haven't got the capacity to understand the answer. In learning to depend on God, we must accept that we may not know all the answers, but we know *who* knows the answers.

YOUR HOPE WILL OVERFLOW

I pray that the God who gives hope will fill you with much joy and peace while you trust in Him. Then your hope will overflow by the power of the Holy Spirit.

Romans 15:13

I've noticed that those who serve God most joyfully are the ones who know Him most personally. Those who are quickest to speak about Jesus are those who realize how great has been their own redemption.

April

April 1

THAT SWEET SURPRISE

This promise is for you, for your children,
and for all who are far away.
It is for everyone the LORD our God calls to Himself.

Acts 2:39

$\mathscr{H}$oly Father, thank You for the sweet surprise of Easter morning. We are thankful that when You arose from Your sleep of death, You didn't go immediately to heaven, but instead You went and visited people. This visit of love reminds us that it was for *people* that You died. We praise Your name for that sweet surprise.

April 2

THE MOST IMMEASURABLE GIFT

This is how we know what real love is:
Jesus gave His life for us. So we should give
our lives for our brothers and sisters.

1 John 3:16

*A*midst all the people at the cruci-
fixion scene there is one person
with whom all of us can identify. We can
all relate to the crucified crook. All of
us hang on the cross beside Jesus. All
of us have made the most unimaginable
request. And all of us who are in the
body of Christ have received the most
unimaginable and immeasurable gift that
we could ever receive – salvation!

SOURCE OF ENERGY

"I am the resurrection and the life.
Those who believe in Me
will have life even if they die."

John 11:25

*E*ach statement made by Jesus on the cross is like a post that we see sometimes on the side of the road that reads "Power Line Buried Here" – and if you dig down, sure enough, you're going to strike power. Those words of Christ are a source of energy into which all of us can tap.

April 4

THE CROSS OF JESUS

Through the cross of Jesus my world
was crucified, and I died to the world.

Galatians 6:14

It wasn't the Romans who nailed
Jesus to the cross. It wasn't the
Jewish religion that took Him up the hill
of Calvary. It wasn't spikes that held
Jesus to the cross. What held Him to
that cross was His conviction that it was
necessary that He become sin – that He
who is pure become sin and that the
wrath of God be poured down, not upon
the creation, but upon the Creator.

April 5

THE DIVINE RELATIONSHIP

But dear friends, use your most holy faith
to build yourselves up, praying in the Holy Spirit.

Jude 20

When Jesus talks about prayer, He doesn't present it as an arduous task, He doesn't describe it as a requirement, He doesn't say that it's something you do beautifully so that some divine audience will throw flowers to you. That's not what prayer is. It's the divine relationship that allows us to stand before God and express the deepest concerns of our hearts.

April 6

WE ARE SET FREE

In Christ we are set free by the
blood of His death, and so we have
forgiveness of sins. How rich is God's grace,
which He has given to us so fully and freely.

Ephesians 1:7–8

When Jesus told us to pray for forgiveness of our debts as we forgive our own debtors, He knew who would be the one to pay the debt. As He would hang on the cross He would say, "It is finished" ... *the debt is paid!*

THE GRACE OF GOD

Christ ended the law so that everyone
who believes in Him may be right with God.

Romans 10:4

What is the grace of God? The grace of God says you serve God *because* you're saved, not in order to *be* saved. You love people *because* you're saved, and not in order to *be* saved. You're not trying to keep a legalistic system, you're responding to a system of love and peace.

April 8

THE SURPRISE PARTY

Mary Magdalene went and said to the followers,
"I saw the Lord!"

John 20:18

If you like surprises, you should like the Bible, because God is the God of surprises. If you like parties, you should like the Bible because God is the God of parties. If you like them both, you should like the story of the surprise party that God gives Mary when she approaches the tomb.

SIMPLY BECAUSE

So you do not belong to yourselves,
because you were bought by God for a price.
1 Corinthians 6:19-20

Our value is inherent – it's not based on the Ph.D. after our name or the amount of money in our bank account. We have value simply because we *are*. In the eyes of God, every human has value simply because he is the creation of the almighty God.

April 10

YOUR GIFT

"I am the light of the world. The person
who follows Me will never live in darkness
but will have the light that gives life."

John 8:12

An itinerant preacher from Naz-
areth can do something for the
hurt that is in your heart. Maybe you're
trying to rebuild an estranged relationship ... Maybe you've been trying to find
God for longer than you can remember.
There was something about this Nazarene
preacher that made people cluster around
Him like He was God's gift to humanity.
He is your gift as well.

April 11

ASKING WHY

No one knows the thoughts of God
except the Spirit of God.

1 Corinthians 2:11

A misconception people have in dealing with life's troubles is that it's wrong to ask why – that a Christian simply accepts and never questions. Abraham, Moses and David all interceded and struggled to understand God. But the lives of these men model for us a total reliance on God, even in the midst of questioning.

April 12

GOD IS LIGHT

God is light, and in Him
there is no darkness at all.
1 John 1:5

Lord, let us not pretend to be something we're not. You know us early in the morning; You know us late at night. You know us when we're weak; You know us when we're strong. Father, remind us that You still care and that You still love us.

April 13

FREE INDEED

Don't depend on your own wisdom.
Respect the Lord and refuse to do wrong.

Proverbs 3:7

Holy God and Father in heaven, we come to You, aware that it's not easy to hear Your voice amidst the manifold voices of the world. Help us realize that You have truly set us free – free from the lures of status and materialism and peer pressure. Help us remember Your promise that when the Son sets us free, we are free indeed.

April 14

THE VOICE OF TRUTH

Let us look only to Jesus, the One who
began our faith and who makes it perfect.

Hebrews 12:2

The Christian is the one who seeks
to discern the voice of God amidst
the many voices that come our way. One
of the greatest challenges that we have
is to learn to hear the voice of truth.

April 15

AN ANCHOR FOR THE SOUL

We have this hope as an anchor for the soul,
sure and strong.

Hebrews 6:19

Nothing and no one can take away God's promise to forgive your sins. Nothing and no one can take away your victory over death. Hold on to your hope, for it is the anchor of your soul.

April 16

SHINE LIKE STARS

The wise people will shine like the brightness
of the sky. Those who teach others to live right
will shine like stars forever and ever.

Daniel 12:3

Do you ever get tired or bored with your work? Christ says turn your work into a ministry — don't let it be just a vocation. Reach out to people. Let your time at work be a source of joy and encouragement to others, and you'll find greater personal joy and satisfaction as well.

THE BEAUTY OF PRAYER

Those who know the LORD trust Him,
because He will not leave those who come to Him.

Psalm 9:10

The beauty of prayer is that anyone can pray. You don't have to be a certain age, you don't have to have wealth, you don't have to have a certain talent – all you have to have is a stubborn faith and willingness to intercede.

THE FIRST GREAT GIFT

But grow in the grace and knowledge
of our Lord and Savior Jesus Christ.
Glory be to Him now and forever! Amen.

2 Peter 3:18

The first great gift God gives His children is His grace. It is a very individually tailored and given gift. Grace is the gift of God's riches: the peace of God, the love of God, the hope of God. We are heirs of God, but at Christ's expense.

April 19

AN UNUSUAL GUEST LIST

And after you suffer for a short time, God,
who gives all grace, will make everything right.
He will make you strong and support you and keep
you from falling. He called you to share in His
glory in Christ, a glory that will continue forever.

1 Peter 5:10

Is there anything that causes you not to have the rest of the Spirit that you need? Jesus issues an invitation to an unusual guest list: those who are tired and overworked, burdened down. Maybe you could put your name on that guest list.

April 20

MADE ALIVE IN THE SPIRIT

Christ Himself suffered for sins once. He was not
guilty, but He suffered for those who are
guilty to bring you to God. His body was killed,
but He was made alive in the spirit.

1 Peter 3:18

When the one who knew no sin
became sin for us, when the
sinless one was covered with all the
sins of all the world, God didn't call His
army of angels to save Him. He didn't,
because He knew He would rather give
up His Son than give up on us.

April 21

THAT PRECIOUS BOOK

I will follow Your rules forever,
because they make me happy.

Psalm 119:111

*F*ather, we're amazed at how practical Your Bible is. Who would have thought that daily help could be found in a book so old. Every time we open it we find it's not old at all. Help us to look for Your guidance in that precious Book.

April 22

HOLY FREEDOM

Grace and peace be given to you
more and more, because you truly
know God and Jesus our Lord.

2 Peter 1:2

*F*ather, help us renew our commit-
ment to You, to release everything
and to be owned and possessed by You.
We long to submit ourselves to You so
that we might know the holy freedom
available to us only through Your grace.

April 23

ENOUGH FAITH

"Why are you afraid?
You don't have enough faith."
Matthew 8:26

Father, as You stilled the storm on the Sea of Galilee, will You still the storms that rage within our hearts? Will You calm the whirling winds of fear and hurt that threaten our faith? Will You, Father, draw us ever closer to You?

April 24

FACE TO FACE

Whoever says that he lives in God
must live as Jesus lived.

1 John 2:6

*J*he apostle Paul gives us the pure
motive for Christian service. If Paul
were here, he'd call us to stand in front
of Christ day after day, knowing that the
longer we stand face to face with Jesus,
the more dynamic our personal lives will
become.

April 25

SAY SO!

Anyone who speaks should speak words from God.
Anyone who serves should serve with the
strength God gives so that in everything God
will be praised through Jesus Christ. Power and
glory belong to Him forever and ever. Amen.

1 Peter 4:11

The psalmist David would tell us
that those who have been redeemed will say so! If we're not saying
so, perhaps it's because we've forgotten
what it is like to be redeemed. Let the
redeemed of the earth say so!

April 26

THE ONLY HONEST RESPONSE

"So go and make followers
of all people in the world."

Matthew 28:19

*T*he only honest response to forgiveness is to speak about it. The
only honest response to God's grace is
then to share it with others. Any other
response is far too timid.

April 27

TEARS LIKE A FLOOD

He was sorry He had made human beings on the earth, and His heart was filled with pain.

Genesis 6:6

Once we see how much God cares for His people, then we begin to see how much His heart must have broken when the hand of man reached out and took the goblet of sin offered by Satan. Because God is perfect, He cannot dwell with a sinful being. He must have wept so much the tears were like a flood and showered the creation.

April 28

SHARING THE NEWS

They praised God and were liked by all the people. Every day the Lord added those who were being saved to the group of believers.

Acts 2:47

There were promises broken at the gate of Gethsemane, and yet, when the disciples fled, they took with them a heart-stopping memory of a man called Jesus. And try as they might, they could not forget Him. The beauty of the story is that they spent the rest of their lives sharing the news of salvation.

April 29

DEAL WITH IT BOLDLY

You can trust God, who will not permit you
to be tempted more than you can stand.

1 Corinthians 10:13

When you think of the temptation with which you struggle most in your life, you can deal with it boldly. You can have the confidence that God has given you a spirit of self-discipline. It's up to you to tap into that gift.

April 30

THE LORD IS KING

The LORD is King forever and ever.
Psalm 10:16

Is there a vacant spot in your heart where there should reside a Savior who died and was resurrected? Do you still have the passion for Jesus that you did years ago? Do you still have the love for the Word that you once did?

May

May 1

RENEW YOUR VISION

"Listen! I am coming soon! I will bring
My reward with Me, and I will repay each
one of you for what you have done."

Revelation 22:12

*F*ather, how holy and great is Your promise. You've been so good to us, but somehow, Father, we find things about which to complain even though we've been given life eternal. Renew our vision; help us to see heaven. Help us to be busy about the right business — the business of serving You.

NO ONE IS USELESS TO GOD

God does not see the same way people see.
People look at the outside of a person,
but the LORD looks at the heart.

1 Samuel 16:7

No one is useless to God. No one, at any point in his life, is useless to God – not a little child, not the unattractive, not the clumsy, not the tired, not the discouraged. God uses His children.

HOW JESUS MUST FEEL

Then the whole town went out to see Jesus.
When they saw Him, they begged
Him to leave their area.

Matthew 8:34

After Jesus cast out the demons, the townspeople were frightened and asked Him to leave. We don't know what Jesus felt, but we can imagine what He felt. If you've ever tried to help somebody and they did not understand your help, maybe you understand how Jesus felt that day. Perhaps you can even understand how Jesus must feel when we reject the One who came to save us.

May 4

WE ARE WAITING

But God made a promise to us, and we
are waiting for a new heaven and
a new earth where goodness lives.

2 Peter 3:13

*F*ather, we know that someday You're going to take all of Your followers into eternal happiness. And it is to that day, Father, that we look. And it is upon our hope and confidence that You will return, that we stand.

May 5

THE IMPORTANCE OF A FRIEND

Whoever loves a brother or sister lives in the light
and will not cause anyone to stumble in his faith.

1 John 2:10

We know the importance of a friend. All of us need friends, don't we? Whether or not you are friendly could determine whether or not someone hears about Jesus Christ. Your handshake, your warmth, your walk, your friendliness could make the difference in someone's life.

May 6

INVITE HIM IN

My dear friends, if our hearts
do not make us feel guilty, we can
come without fear into God's presence.

1 John 3:21

*R*un to Jesus. Jesus wants you to go to Him. He wants to become the most important person in your life, the greatest love you'll ever know. He wants you to love Him so much that there's no room in your heart and in your life for sin. Invite Him to take up residence in your heart.

May 7

HAVE COURAGE

Be alert. Continue strong in the faith.
Have courage, and be strong.

1 Corinthians 16:13

We don't look like we're afraid, Father – calm on the outside. But Father, we have our hidden fears. You know them. We're afraid of being alone. We're afraid of being jobless. We're afraid of pain. Father, we offer these fears to You, and ask You to give us more courage as we look at You, the One who knows no fear.

May 8

YOU WERE CHOSEN

But you are a chosen people, royal priests, a holy nation, a people for God's own possession. You were chosen to tell about the wonderful acts of God, who called you out of darkness into His wonderful light.

1 Peter 2:9

As Christians, we symbolize the belief that Jesus is the Son of God. Perhaps for some that belief is hidden or almost forgotten. And yet, for many, that belief is vibrant and fruitful. Whatever the condition of our belief, may God daily show us Jesus and Him only. May we constantly see our redemption and then in turn proclaim it. How great and sweet is the name of Jesus!

May 9

FOOLING OURSELVES

So if we say we have fellowship with God, but we
continue living in darkness, we are liars and do not
follow the truth ... If we say we have no sin, we
are fooling ourselves, and the truth is not in us.

1 John 1:6, 8

We Western-culture-type folks like to deal with things we can see and hold, but when we talk about something from another source, we're uneasy. When something doesn't fit our mentality, we give it a new paradigm – instead of calling evil "Satan", we call evil "the lack of welfare" or "the lack of education." If we can blame Satan's fruits on heredity or heritage, he doesn't seem so mean.

May 10

I CALL YOU FRIENDS

"I no longer call you servants, because a servant does not know what his master is doing. But I call you friends, because I have made known to you everything I heard from My Father."

John 15:15

Jesus described for His followers what He came to do. He came to build a relationship with people. He came to take away enmity, to take away the strife, to take away the isolation that existed between God and man. Once He bridged that, once He overcame that, He said, "I will call you friends."

May 11

GOD'S MERCY

At one time, you were not a people, but now you are God's people. In the past you had never received mercy, but now you have received God's mercy.

1 Peter 2:10

Man walks a slim line clearly symbolized by the life of Paul – on one side of the line was his utter failure. On the other side of the line was the only thing deeper than his failure – the grace of Christ.

May 12

GOD REMEMBERS

So do not lose the courage you had in the past, which has a great reward. You must hold on, so you can do what God wants and receive what He has promised.

Hebrews 10:35-36

*D*o you ever wonder if everything will turn out right as long as you do everything right? Do you ever try to do something right and yet nothing seems to turn out like you planned? Take heart – when people do what is right, God remembers.

May 13

USE TIME WISELY

Plant goodness, harvest the fruit of loyalty, plow the new ground of knowledge. Look for the LORD until He comes and pours goodness on you like water.

Hosea 10:12

Father, help us to use our time wisely, to take advantage of the opportunities we have to be just the type of Christians You want us to be. When it seems like we don't have enough time to do what we need to do, increase our gratitude for the challenges of each day. And help us meet those challenges in ways that please You.

ALLOW GOD TO HELP

So those who suffer as God wants
should trust their souls to the faithful Creator
as they continue to do what is right.

1 Peter 4:19

Something happens to us when we struggle with physical or emotional or financial problems. Either we can become paralyzed by our problems, turning inward and getting hooked on the "angel dust" of pity, or we can defeat the inclination to turn inward, and allow God to help us grow through these difficulties.

GRACE IS A FREE GIFT

Everyone has sinned and fallen short of God's
glorious standard, and all need to be made right
with God by His grace, which is a free gift.

Romans 3:23-24

What is grace? It's what someone
gives us out of the goodness of
their hearts, not out of the perfection of
ours. The story of grace is the good
news that says that when we come, He
gives. That's what grace is.

May 16

MOTHERHOOD

She watches over her family and never wastes
her time. Her children speak well of her.

Proverbs 31:27-28

There's something inherent about
the qualities of motherhood that
would cause anyone who questioned the
existence of God to be convinced. What
is it about motherhood that gives women
six sets of hands, three pairs of eyes,
a body with 180 parts, all replaceable,
and the capacity to get by on coffee and
leftovers?

SERVING OUT OF LOVE

Your rules are wonderful. That is why I keep them.
Learning Your words gives wisdom
and understanding for the foolish.

Psalm 119:129-130

When you light somebody afire with the grace of God, you have a hard time putting him out. When you light people with legalism or with rules and regulations, they're going to burn out because they'll always live in fear. But a person set afire with the love of Jesus Christ will live in gratitude serving his Lord out of love and not out of fear.

May 18

VALUABLE QUALITIES

But the Spirit produces the fruit of
love, joy, peace, patience, kindness, goodness,
faithfulness, gentleness, self-control.

Galatians 5:22-23

There are no perfect mothers. There
are no perfect people. But someone in Scripture who teaches some valuable
qualities we need as servants of God is
Mary. She reminds us that God uses those
who are willing, thoughtful, loyal, and faithful.

May 19

GOD'S POWER

God's power protects you through your faith until
salvation is shown to you at the end of time.

1 Peter 1:5

The power of a strong relationship
sustains us and gives us strength –
it's that power in knowing, *If I fail, my
friend is still there, or, If I fail, I have a
wife who still loves me*. It's the power in
knowing that – no matter what – we have
a Father who still loves us.

May 20

BLESS THE MOTHERS

Happy are those who respect the LORD and obey Him.
You will enjoy what you work for,
and you will be blessed with good things.

Psalm 128:12

*F*ather, bless the mothers of our world. As we think of the hands that guided us and those who are now guiding young lives, we stand before You on their behalf, in gratefulness and anticipation. And, Father, we pray a special prayer for those who yearn to be mothers but have yet to be graced with that child, asking for Your special care and blessing on them.

May 21

STRENGTHEN YOURSELVES

Since Christ suffered while He was in His body,
strengthen yourselves with the same way
of thinking Christ had. The person who
has suffered in the body is finished with sin.

1 Peter 4:1

As Jesus looked down from the cross, who did He see? He saw a loyal mother. To us, this was a moment of glory, but to Mary, it was the moment of her greatest pain. She was there, at that very last moment, to give that final word of strength, to weep that final maternal tear as her child made that final sacrifice.

May 22

GREAT THINGS

The LORD has done great things for us,
and we are very glad.

Psalm 126:3

What have we ever done to deserve the healing touch of Jesus to our souls? Nothing! Yet often we come to Jesus feeling pretty good about ourselves, saying, "Hey, I'll make a great contribution to Your team." Hogwash! Jesus doesn't need us on His team. And He doesn't forgive us on the basis of what we've done. He forgives us on the basis of who He is.

May 23

MADE RIGHT

Being made right with God by His grace, we could have the hope of receiving the life that never ends.

Titus 3:7

Do you wonder where you can go for encouragement and motivation? Go back to that moment when you first saw the love of Jesus Christ. Remember the day when you were separated from Christ? You knew only guilt and confusion and then – a light. Someone opened a door and light came into your darkness, and you said in your heart, "I am redeemed!"

May 24

SPECIAL PONDERING

Now, my children, listen to me, because
those who follow my ways are happy.

Proverbs 8:32

*P*raying for our children is a noble
task. If what we are doing in
this fast-paced society is taking us away
from prayer time for our children, we're
doing too much. There is nothing more
special, more precious than that time that
a parent spends struggling and pondering
with God on behalf of a child.

May 25

NOT GUILTY!

Through Christ Jesus the law of the Spirit
that brings life made you free from
the law that brings sin and death.

Romans 8:2

oes the Word of God say, "There
is *limited* condemnation for those
who are in Christ Jesus"? No. Does it
say, "There is *some* condemnation ... "?
No. It says, "There is *no* condemnation
for those who are in Christ Jesus." Think
of it – regardless of our sin, we are not
guilty!

May 26

LIBERATING GRACE

God's grace has made me what I am,
and His grace to me was not wasted.

1 Corinthians 15:10

You know what happens when someone sees the grace of God? When
someone really tastes the forgiving and
liberating grace of God? Someone who
tastes God's grace is the hardest worker,
the most morally pure individual, and the
person most willing to forgive.

May 27

THE TENDER-HEARTED JESUS

When Jesus saw Mary crying and
the Jews who came with her also crying,
He was upset and was deeply troubled.

John 11:33

Most of the people in the world have never seen the Jesus of the New Testament – a Redeemer whose eyes would swell with tears and whose heart would beat with passion. Most people serve a Redeemer only when they need a favor – a sort of magic Lord who's ignored except in time of crisis. We can't imitate a magic Jesus. The tender-hearted Jesus of the New Testament demands imitation by those who follow Him.

May 28

INTERESTED IN OUR PAIN

"This man was born blind so that
God's power could be shown in him."

John 9:3

Jesus and His disciples saw a blind man while walking down the road. The disciples said, "Jesus, who sinned?" Jesus said, "No one sinned." Then Jesus healed the man. And He eternally answered that our pain is not a result of our sin. God is not so small that He would zap us for making a mistake. This passage teaches just the opposite: Our Savior is not asleep; Jesus is alive and interested in our pain.

May 29

GUIDE US

"But be faithful, even if you have to die,
and I will give you the crown of life."

Revelation 2:10

O Father, for the surety that there is a truth in this world, we're thankful. For the assurance that there is a right and a wrong and that You have always done what is right, we're thankful. We've all failed You; we've all taken wrong paths and made wrong choices. Guide us, Father. Enrich our conscience so that we may be faithful to the great and wonderful gift You've given us.

May 30

WAITING TO EMBRACE US

As the mountains surround Jerusalem,
the LORD surrounds His people now and forever.

Psalm 125:2

We have a Father who is filled with compassion, a feeling Father who hurts when His children hurt. We serve a God who says that even when we're under pressure and feel like nothing is going to go right, He's waiting for us, to embrace us whether we succeed or fail.

May 31

ALL EQUALITY AVAILABLE

I wait for the LORD to help me,
and I trust His word.

Psalm 130:5

When Jesus told the story of the missing sheep, some of the people who were listening wiped away a tear because they knew how it feels to be lost among the crowd. Jesus wanted us to understand that we have a Father who sees and cares for each one of His children — that we are all equally valuable to Him.

June

June 1

A PARENT'S PLEAS

Can't the creator of ears hear?
Can't the maker of eyes see?

Psalm 94:9

Never underestimate the ponderings of a Christian parent. Never underestimate the power that comes when a parent pleads with God on behalf of a child. Who knows how many prayers are being answered right now because of the faithful ponderings of a parent ten or twenty years ago? God listens to thoughtful parents.

June 2

DOING WHAT'S RIGHT

LORD, let me live so people will praise You.
Psalm 143:11

Do what is right this week, whatever it is, whatever comes down the path, whatever problems and dilemmas you face – just do what's right. Maybe no one else is doing what's right, but you do what's right. You be honest. You take a stand. You be true. After all, regardless of what you do, God does what is right: He saves you with His grace.

June 3

NO SIN TOO DEEP

Keep yourselves in God's love as you
wait for the Lord Jesus Christ with
His mercy to give you life forever.

Jude 21

*F*ather, we want to come home to
You. But sometimes we're afraid
that we've done something unforgivable,
afraid that we've made You angry. And
we wonder how You can forgive us. But
Father, Your Word teaches us that You
will forgive us and that there's no sin
too deep for Your hand of forgiveness
to reach.

June 4

JOY WITH TROUBLE

We also have joy with our troubles, because we
know that these troubles produce patience.

Romans 5:3

*S*ometimes people question God –
"Is pain my punishment?" You've
heard the expression "The rain falls on the
just and the unjust" – or better, the unjust
and the unjust, for we are all sinners. All
of us are or will be victims of pain – it's
simply a fact of our existence, regardless
of how good or how bad we are. Life isn't
fair? No, but there is One who justifies
life and understands that pain.

THAT BRIDGE OF FRIENDSHIP

Love means living the way God commanded us to live.
As you have heard from the beginning,
His command is this: Live a life of love.

2 John 1:6

We're in a fast-moving, fast-paced society. We need to build bridges between our hearts and those of people we see who need a friend – and allow Jesus to cross that bridge of friendship and walk into their hearts.

June 6

HIS HEALING HAND

The LORD helps those who have been defeated
and takes care of those who are in trouble.

Psalm 145:14

hen Jesus healed the woman in Matthew 9, He told her that her faith had made her well. He was also saying to her, "You're very special to Me, daughter. I know you don't have anything to offer Me; I know you've been rejected by society, but your Father has not forgotten you." Our Savior says the same to us when we need His healing hand.

June 7

DEFEAT EVIL

Do not let evil defeat you,
but defeat evil by doing good.

Romans 12:21

*F*ather, when we confront temptation, when we stand face to face
with evil, we pray that You would give
us strength and that You would use Your
power to block the path of evil.

A CLEAR CONSCIENCE

Keep a clear conscience so that
those who speak evil of your good life
in Christ will be made ashamed.

1 Peter 3:16

*U*nresolved guilt is fatal. Unresolved mistakes kill. And they don't just kill you, they kill others. Unresolved errors cause us to do what is illogical, cause us to explode at someone who is innocent, cause someone who has not participated in the sin to receive the consequences.

June 9

RIGHT HERE!

My friends, do not be surprised at the terrible trouble which now comes to test you. Do not think that something strange is happening to you. But be happy that you are sharing in Christ's sufferings so that you will be happy and full of joy when Christ comes again in glory.

1 Peter 4:12-13

Where is God when we hurt? Where is He when sleep won't come? Where is He when we awaken in a hospital bed with pain that won't subside? He's right here! He hung on the gallows to prove once and for all that He's here – that He didn't create the hurt, but He came to take it away.

June 10

YOUR ENEMY –
THE EVIL ONE

The devil, your enemy, goes around like
a roaring lion looking for someone to eat.

1 Peter 5:8

We should recognize who Satan is and not be afraid to point a finger at him. He is our enemy, and if we understand who the enemy is, we can better arm ourselves against him. The enemy in your marriage is not your spouse. The enemy at your work is not your employer or your employee. The enemy is not the system and not the church. The enemy is the evil one.

June 11

LEARNING HOW
TO TRUST GOD

I was put to death on the cross with Christ,
and I do not live anymore – it is Christ who lives in me.
I still live in my body, but I live by faith in the Son of
God who loved me and gave Himself to save me.

Galatians 2:20

It seems to me that learning how to trust God defines the meaning of Christian living. God doesn't wait until we have our moral lives in order before He starts loving us. This is the inexpressible love of God.

June 12

THE FAITHFUL WITNESS

Jesus is the faithful witness, the first among those raised from the dead. He is the ruler of the kings of the earth. He is the One who loves us, who made us free from our sins with the blood of His death.

Revelation 1:5

I want you to know something. When you hurt, God hurts with you. When no one listens to you, God listens to you. When you wipe away tears of loneliness or frustration or anguish, in heaven there's a pierced hand approaching, a heavenly face wiping away a tear.

June 13

A SPIRIT OF POWER

God did not give us a spirit that makes us afraid
but a spirit of power and love and self-control.

2 Timothy 1:7

*G*od can take that which no one else
would use and empower it like no
one else can.

June 14

A DIFFERENT KIND OF FREEDOM

Live as free people, but do not use your freedom
as an excuse to do evil. Live as servants of God.

1 Peter 2:16

*F*reedom is an elusive thing – it's the carrot on the end of the stick that causes a lot of us mules to do the things we do. Jesus spoke of freedom, but He spoke of a different kind of freedom: the type of freedom that comes not through power but through submission. Not through control but through surrender. Not through possessions but through open hands.

June 15

TO BE FAITHFUL

"I am the One who searches hearts and minds,
and I will repay each of you
for what you have done."

Revelation 2:23

The task of fatherhood is to be faithful to the heavenly Father, to the spouse that God has given him, and to his children. If a father goes to his grave a pauper but is faithful on those three levels, he is a successful man.

WHAT SWEETER BLESSING

Finally, all of you should be in agreement,
understanding each other, loving each other as family,
being kind and humble.

1 Peter 3:8

God blessed the commandment to honor our father and mother. He blessed it with a promise — a promise of joy, a promise of faithfulness. For what sweeter blessing is there than a family whose members shower honor on one another!

June 17

PREPARE YOUR HEARTS

Look, Jesus is coming with the clouds,
and everyone will see Him.

Revelation 1:7

*F*olks, if you're expecting to be given a fair shake in your life, forget it! You won't be. You're going to face illness. And your body is going to wear out. You may be the victim of someone else's mistake. But you can get through those tough times if you prepare your heart now, living to know and serve the Savior who loves you and died so that you might have an eternal home free of pain and sorrow.

June 18

FAITHFUL LOVE

"I want faithful love more than I want
animal sacrifices. I want people to know
Me more than I want burnt offerings."

Hosea 6:6

God loves those who need Him most,
who rely on Him, depend on Him,
and trust Him in everything. Little He
cares whether you've been as pure as
John or as sinful as Mary Magdalene; all
that matters is your trust in Him.

June 19

BOLDNESS IN GOD'S PRESENCE

And this is the boldness we have in God's presence:
that if we ask God for anything that
agrees with what He wants, He hears us.
If we know He hears us every time we ask Him,
we know we have what we ask from Him.

1 John 5:14–15

*F*ather, help us today to maintain our promise of faithfulness to You, even in times when we're not surrounded by people who agree with us and encourage and understand our devotion to You. Give us great courage as we face the challenges of each new day.

June 20

COMFORTING OTHERS

He comforts us every time we have trouble,
so when others have trouble, we can comfort
them with the same comfort God gives us.

2 Corinthians 1:4

*S*truggling with life's difficulties makes us a little wiser, a little more capable, enabling us to comfort others who experience pain.

June 21

A GESTURE OF AFFECTION

Do everything in love.

1 Corinthians 16:14

*N*ever underestimate a gesture of affection. What you consider as wasted gestures may be the very thing that your child will never forget. If your child remembers anything, let him remember the tender affection that you had for him as a child.

June 22

A CERTAIN HUMILITY

Pride will ruin people,
but those who are humble will be honored.

Proverbs 29:23

I am frightened by our ability in America to convince ourselves that we don't need Jesus. We can amass fortunes, we can get degrees, we can own our house all on our own. And yet, there's a certain affluence that we can attain when we become poverty-stricken – a certain humility that comes with trials, that brings us face to face with the Savior.

June 23

THE KINGDOM OF HEAVEN

He made us to be a kingdom of priests
who serve God His Father. To Jesus Christ
be glory and power forever and ever! Amen.

Revelation 1:6

The Gospel is an easily understand-able and transmittable message. The whole Gospel can be brought down to one phrase: The kingdom of heaven is near! There's a King and there's a kingdom, and you can be a part of it. The choice is yours.

June 24

GOD'S LOVE FOR YOU

Holy, holy, holy is the Lord God Almighty.
He was, He is, and He is coming.

Revelation 4:8

God's love for you is not dependent on how you look, how you think, how you act, or how perfect you are. His love is absolutely non-negotiable and non-returnable. Ours is a faithful God.

June 25

SET YOUR PRIORITIES

So prepare your minds for service and have self-control. All your hope should be for the gift of grace that will be yours when Jesus Christ is shown to you.

1 Peter 1:13

*S*ometimes life gets confusing, doesn't it? Do you wake up with a list of things to do that is far longer than the hours you have? To set your priorities, find an answer to this question: Where do you want to be 100 years from now? If your answer is heaven, then your daily choices will have only one criteria: getting there!

June 26

GENUINE REPENTANCE

"If My people, who are called by My name,
will humble themselves, if they will pray and seek Me
and stop their evil ways, I will hear them from heaven.
I will forgive their sin, and I will heal their land."

2 Chronicles 7:14

Genuine repentance is a moving condition of the heart that is testified and demonstrated by our deeds. It's an inward conviction that expresses itself in outward actions.

June 27

DEMONSTRATE YOUR DEVOTION

Do what you learned and received from me,
what I told you, and what you saw me do.
And the God who gives peace will be with you.

Philippians 4:9

Oftentimes we say one thing and we do another. Paul, the apostle, says that all Christians are letters from Christ. People look at how you act before they look at what you say. We must demonstrate our devotion to Christ.

June 28

EMBRACE US FATHER

If I rise with the sun in the east and settle in the
west beyond the sea, even there You would guide me.
With Your right hand You would hold me.

Psalm 139:9-10

God of heaven, we see Your hand
stretching as far as the east is from
the west. Put Your hands and Your arms
around us and embrace us, Father. Take
us home. May we be Yours forever.

June 29

HE IS THE WAY

But if anyone does sin, we have a helper
in the presence of the Father – Jesus Christ,
the One who does what is right.
He died in our place to take away our sins,
and not only our sins but the sins of all people.

1 John 2:1–2

What makes a Christian a Christian
is not perfection but forgiveness.

June 30

FAN THE FLAME

"Here I am! I stand at the door and knock. If you hear My voice and open the door, I will come in and eat with you, and you will eat with Me."

Revelation 3:20

Can you recall the moment you first believed? You felt a flame in your heart that was dancing so hot that you knew even death couldn't put it out. Is that flame still there? If it is, then fan it, bring it to life. Stand face to face with the only hope this earth knows.

July

July 1

IT'S NOT TOO LATE

Lord, even when I have trouble all around me,
You will keep me alive.
When my enemies are angry, You will
reach down and save me by Your power.

Psalm 138:7

Regardless of what you've done, it's not too late. Regardless of how far you've fallen, it's not too late. It doesn't matter how low the mistake is, it's not too late to dig down, pull out that mistake, and let it go — and be free.

July 2

"I'LL GIVE YOU ETERNITY"

"God did not send His Son into the world to judge the
world guilty, but to save the world through Him."

John 3:17

*E*ven if you've fallen, even if you've
failed, even if everyone else has
rejected you, Christ will not turn away
from you. He came first and foremost to
those who have no hope. He goes to
those no one else would go to and says,
"I'll give you eternity."

DON'T BE TOO PROUD

Humble yourself in the Lord's presence,
and He will honor you.

James 4:10

Indifference stirs the wrath of God: indifferent people who have grown spiritually dull, who are unresponsive, who see their own sinfulness and yet never fall to their knees and say, "I'm sorry, God."

July 4

RELEASED FROM THAT BONDAGE

He will bring about what is right for me.
Then He will bring me out into the light,
and I will see Him set things right.

Micah 7:9

We enjoy many freedoms in the United States. But unless you've been freed by God Almighty, there is one bondage you still carry, regardless of the country you're in. And that's the freedom of yesterday's regrets, yesterday's failures. All of us need to have that capacity and strength to stand tall with confidence that God has released us from that bondage of regret.

July 5

REALIZE THE URGENCY

"So be eager to do right,
and change your hearts and lives."

Revelation 3:19

What's the difference between a Christian who's reaching out to people, trying to help people – and a Christian who sits like a fat cat on a pew? Well, maybe the Christian who's reaching out realizes the urgency and re- members what it was like before he knew about Jesus. Maybe he realizes that when people need help, they need Jesus above all else.

July 6

A SINCERE REGRET

On the day I called to You, You answered me.
You made me strong and brave.

Psalm 138:3

No one is happier than the one who has sincerely repented of wrong. Repentance is the decision to turn from selfish desires and seek God. It is a genuine, sincere regret that creates sorrow and moves us to admit wrong and desire to do better.

July 7

WE TAKE HOPE

His glory covers the skies, and His praise fills the earth.
He is like a bright light. Rays of light shine
from His hand, and there He hides His power.

Habakkuk 3:3-4

*F*ather, You never promised us that this world would be easy. And yet, all of us can look ahead to the city that's set on a hill, to the lights that call us to eternity. And we take hope.

July 8

LORD, I WILL THANK YOU

LORD, I will thank You with all my heart;
I will sing to You.

Psalm 138:1

It's incredible that anyone could look at the kindness of God, the faithfulness of God, and the goodness of God and not feel any emotion of gratitude.

July 9

LISTEN AS GOD TEACHES

The LORD corrects those He loves, just as
parents correct the child they delight in.

Proverbs 3:12

The struggles that you're going through now – don't discard them. Listen to God as He teaches you so that you can teach others. You see, a time of suffering teaches us something we never knew before and may prepare us for a time of counsel that we will give some-one years from now.

LIFE'S BATTLEGROUND

Our fight is not against people on earth
but against the rulers and authorities and
the powers of this world's darkness, against the
spiritual powers of evil in the heavenly world.

Ephesians 6:12

Where's our battleground in life? Is our battle against our neighbor? Is our battle against our family? No. The battle is with the invisible forces of evil, the black one that has invaded the earth, whose goal is to win the battle within every Christian. Satan failed in his desire to control God, and it's only with God's help that we can defeat him.

CLARIFY WHAT YOUR TASK IS

Always be ready to answer everyone who asks you to explain about the hope you have.

1 Peter 3:15

Do you want to simplify your life? Then clarify what your task is. What are the words, what are the concepts, what message do you want to transmit to your friends and family? The truth of Jesus Christ is the simple truth of His sacrifice.

July 12

THE LORD IS GOOD

The LORD is good, giving protection in times of trouble.
He knows who trusts in Him.

Nahum 1:7

A lot of us live with a hidden fear that God is angry at us. Somewhere, sometime, some Sunday school class or some television show convinced us that God has a whip behind His back, a paddle in His back pocket, and He's going to nail us when we've gone too far. No concept could be more wrong! Your Savior's Father is very fond of you and only wants to share His love with you.

July 13

THE ROAD TO EVERLASTING LIFE

See if there is any bad thing in me.
Lead me on the road to everlasting life.

Psalm 139:24

Father in heaven, help us as we cope and grapple with yesterday's failures. They dog at our heels like irritations. They follow us around. They cling to our ankles like fifteen-pound ball weights. Help us to release those regrets in the right way, and keep us close.

July 14

THE VOICE OF GOD

God, Your thoughts are precious to me.
They are so many! If I could count them,
they would be more than all the grains of sand.
When I wake up, I am still with You.

Psalm 139:17-18

*R*ecreation rebuilds the interior of man. It's not just getting out and playing golf; it's being so silent that you can hear the voice of God.

July 15

THE FIRE THAT CAN'T BE PUT OUT

The LORD will be King forever.
Jerusalem, your God is everlasting. Praise the LORD!

Psalm 146:10

Those who have been redeemed just can't keep quiet. There's something about the fire that burns in their hearts that even the winds of secularism and humanism and peer pressure just can't put it out.

July 16

BORN AGAIN

You have been born again, and this new life
did not come from something that dies, but from
something that cannot die. You were born again
through God's living message that continues forever.

1 Peter 1:23

When a Christian becomes a follower of Christ, he dies to himself.
And the life that he possesses is the life to
come, not this life on earth.

July 17

GOOD REIGNS SUPREME

God, You have heard my promises.
You have given me what belongs
to those who fear You.

Psalm 61:5

*F*ather, thank You for Your promise that if we do what is right, eventually truth and justice and goodness will prevail. As we face the dilemmas and options of this time, remind us that good does reign supreme.

July 18

TREASURES IN HEAVEN

"Store your treasures in heaven where they cannot be destroyed by moths or rust and where thieves cannot break in and steal them."

Matthew 6:20

The kingdom never advances because of our possessions. It advances because of our faith. "Lean on Me," says Jesus. He needs us to depend on Him rather than on our possessions.

July 19

TOSS IT AWAY

"Though your sins are like scarlet,
they can be white as snow. Though your sins
are deep red, they can be white like wool."

Isaiah 1:18

Sometimes we try to deal with a mistake by covering it up with more mistakes, or by repressing it, or by justifying it. That's like walking around with a pebble in our shoe – it causes us so much frustration that our whole body compensates for its presence, when all we have to do is take it out and toss it away.

July 20

GIVE, AND YOU WILL RECEIVE

"Give, and you will receive. You will be given much.
Pressed down, shaken together, and running over,
it will spill into your lap. The way you give
to others is the way God will give to you."

Luke 6:38

*G*od doesn't want us because of what we have to offer Him He wants us because *He* has everything to offer *us*. God doesn't want you because you have certain gifts to offer. He wants to give you gifts so that you then can offer them to other people.

July 21

THE PURITY OF YOUR FAITH

The purity of your faith will bring
you praise and glory and honor
when Jesus Christ is shown to you.

1 Peter 1:7

*F*ather, we believe that when we see
You, any suffering that we endured
on the face of this earth will be worth it.
We believe that the first five minutes we
stand in heaven we will know that anything we endured on this globe will be
forgotten. Father, help us to understand.
And when we cannot understand, help us
to trust.

July 22

TELL THE GOOD NEWS

"Go everywhere in the world,
and tell the Good News to everyone."

Mark 16:15

*T*he most important thing we can do on this earth is reach out and help those who have not yet found the key to that life that is to come.

July 23

GOD CALLS US TO PRAY

The LORD is close to everyone who prays
to Him, to all who truly pray to Him.

Psalm 145:18

*W*hen God says to pray, He really means it. To pray is the most commonly mentioned command in Scripture. It is mentioned more than "love your neighbor," more than "go to church," and more than "evangelize." More than anything else, God calls us to pray.

July 24

ALL OF THAT AND MORE!

Amen! Praise, glory, wisdom, thanks, honor, power, and strength belong to our God forever and ever. Amen!

Revelation 7:12

Father, had You not become flesh and dwelt among us, had You not treated us with mercy and kindness, had You not loved us beyond our worth, You'd still be God. You'd still be worthy of our praise. And You'd still be holy. Yet, Father, You did all of that and more.

July 25

TIMELESS TRUTHS

Don't make me either rich or poor;
just give me enough food for each day.
If I have too much, I might reject You and say,
"I don't know the LORD." If I am poor,
I might steal and disgrace the name of my God.

Proverbs 30:8-9

*F*ather, help us to see what is important, what is eternal, and what is lasting. Let us make decisions based on our eternal life and not on temporary possessions. Father, help us to put into practice the timeless truths found in Your Word. And most of all, Father, thank You for loving us.

July 26

FORGIVE EACH OTHER

Bear with each other, and forgive each other.
If someone does wrong to you, forgive that
person because the Lord forgave you.

Colossians 3:13

Jesus says, "Use your head, but don't lower your standards." You be the one who interrupts that vicious cycle of paying one another back. Don't get on the roller coaster of resentment and anger. You be the one who says, "Yes, he mistreated me, but I am going to be like Christ. I'll be the one who says, 'Forgive them, Father, they don't know what they're doing.'"

July 27

STAND STRONG IN THE LORD

My dear brothers and sisters, I love you and want to
see you. You bring me joy and make me proud of you,
so stand strong in the Lord as I have told you.

Philippians 4:1

A Christian in his surroundings
should encourage everyone to
be better, instead of being the one who
stoops to be like everyone else.

July 28

HOPE IS THE ANCHOR
FOR YOUR SOUL

Through Christ you believe in God, who raised
Christ from the dead and gave Him glory.
So your faith and your hope are in God.

1 Peter 1:21

Our hope is the anchor for the soul. "Where's your hope?" Jesus asks. It is the confident hope of the return of Christ.

July 29

"DO NOT WORRY"

I have taken Your words to heart
so I would not sin against You.

Psalm 119:11

$\mathcal{T}$he same God that gave us commandments such as "Do not commit adultery, do not murder" said, "Do not worry." It's a violation of our relationship to God to question His authority by worrying.

July 30

LORD, HEAR MY PRAYER

LORD, hear my prayer, and listen when I ask
for mercy. I call to You in times of trouble,
because You will answer me.

Psalm 86:6-7

*N*obody else on the face of the
earth is praying to God except
Christians. That's why Christians must be
about the business of intercessory prayer.
When we encounter battles and struggles in life, the first step of the Christian
is to pray. Every time we pray about
something, every time we sincerely take
something to God, God handles it, and
God deals with it.

July 31

WITH THE HOPE PROMISED US

If you are beaten for doing wrong, there is
no reason to praise you for being patient in your
punishment. But if you suffer for doing good,
and you are patient, then God is pleased.

1 Peter 2:20

*S*ometimes it seems when we try to do something good, the more bad things happen, doesn't it? It's tough to have problems when you are trying to be a faithful servant of God, or trying to be loyal to your family. Life was not designed to be problem free, but with the hope promised us by the Father, we can handle the problems that come into our daily lives.

August

August 1

PURE LIKE CHRIST

Christ is pure, and all who have this hope
in Christ keep themselves pure like Christ.

1 John 3:3

*G*od says you're on your way to
becoming a disciple when you can
keep a clear head and a pure heart.

August 2

GRACIOUS TO US

You are worthy, our Lord and God,
to receive glory and honor and power,
because You made all things. Everything
existed and was made, because You wanted it.

Revelation 4:11

*F*ather in heaven, hear our praise. Holy Father, we are thankful that we have more than enough clothes to wear, thankful that we have places to sleep and that we won't go to bed hungry. We're thankful that even if all of this were taken away from us, we'd still have our hope of eternity. You have been gracious to us.

THE LORD GOD IS MY STRENGTH

The Lord GOD is my strength.
He makes me like a deer that does not stumble
so I can walk on the steep mountains.

Habakkuk 3:19

As long as we have hope, as long as we recognize that this world is not our home, as long as we recognize that someday all of our problems will be solved, that is where we will gather our strength.

WALK THROUGH THAT DOOR

"You will not succeed by your own strength
or by your own power, but by My Spirit,"
says the LORD All-Powerful.

Zechariah 4:6

*G*od has opened a door for you. Now you can choose to spend the rest of your life enslaved by guilt and remorse, or you can walk through that door and close it behind you.

August 5

GOD KNOWS YOUR NAME

I will bow down facing Your holy Temple, and I will
thank You for Your love and loyalty. You have made
Your name and Your word greater than anything.

Psalm 138:2

*D*oesn't it feel good when people remember your name? I really appreciate it when people remember my name. I used to wonder why God would have all those lists of people's names in the Bible. The answer is that those names are important to God – He knows all those names, just as He knows yours and mine.

August 6

WRITTEN IN YOUR BOOK

All the days planned for me were written
in Your book before I was one day old.

Psalm 139:16

You know, we really don't know what to pray for, do we? What if God had answered every prayer that you ever prayed? Just think who you'd be married to. Just think where you'd be living. Just think what you'd be doing.

August 7

FORGIVE OUR DOUBTS

LORD, You do everything for me.
LORD, Your love continues forever.

Psalm 138:8

*F*ather, forgive us for the times that we have questioned You; forgive us for the times we have doubted You; forgive us for the times we've shaken our heads and pounded our fists against the earth and cried, "Where are You?" For Father, we know that You have been here – You've carried us through the valley and You've given us strength.

GRAB THAT ANCHOR OF THE SOUL

You are receiving the goal of your faith –
the salvation of your souls.

1 Peter 1:9

One thing no one can take away from you is your faith. This world can and may take everything you have. But no one can take away your faith. Grab that faith; clutch tightly that anchor of the soul.

August 9

GOD FORGIVES
ALL OUR MISTAKES

God, examine me and know my heart;
test me and know my anxious thoughts.

Psalm 139:23

*R*evealing our feelings is the beginning of healing. Articulating
what's on our hearts, confessing our
mistakes, is the first step in seeing that
God can forgive those mistakes and all
others.

August 10

OUR GUIDE THROUGH LIFE

The LORD your God is with you;
the mighty One will save you.
He will rejoice over you. You will rest in His love;
He will sing and be joyful about you.

Zephaniah 3:17

*F*ather, we invite You to be our guide through life. Lord, we don't ask that You take from us the worries of this life but that You surface the worries of this life so that we can share them with You and turn them over to You.

August 11

AN ANCHOR IN
THE LAND TO COME

"At that time I will gather you; at that time I will
bring you back home. I will give you honor and praise
from people everywhere when I make things go well
again for you, as you will see with your own eyes."

Zephaniah 3:20

Within each of us is a desire to
know what lies ahead, a desire
to have hope, a desire to have an anchor
cast in the land to come so that we can
endure the land of today.

August 12

RECOGNIZE THE GIVER

Fear God and give Him praise, because the
time has come for God to judge all people.
So worship God who made the heavens, and
the earth, and the sea, and the springs of water.

Revelation 14:7

Isn't it ironic that times of trouble remind us that we live by God's blessings and not by our own goodness? We grow accustomed to our blessings so much that when our blessings aren't there, we begin to truly recognize them and the Giver as well.

August 13

WE GIVE YOU PRAISE

Yes, God made all things, and everything
continues through Him and for Him.
To Him be the glory forever! Amen.

Romans 11:36

Dear Father, we give You praise. We honor and glorify Your name. You truly are the King of kings and the Lord of lords. We thank You and worship You and glorify Your name forever and ever.

PUT YOUR ANXIETIES ON HIM

Give all your worries to Him,
because He cares about you.

1 Peter 5:7

*G*od wants you to put your anxieties on Him. Let Him do your worrying for you because He is faithful. When you read this verse, substitute your own name for the word *you*. Isn't that good to hear?

August 15

NO MORE PAIN

He will wipe away every tear from their eyes,
and there will be no more death, sadness, crying,
or pain, because all the old ways are gone.

Revelation 21:4

*F*ather, You never said there would
be a day with no rain. You never
said there would be life with no pain. But
You did promise that if we would endure,
we would be saved.

August 16

GOD'S PURPOSE

"I will make My people strong,
and they will live as I say," says the LORD.

Zechariah 10:12

There is an eternal purpose. There is a great river of God's purpose that is moving toward an eternal home with Him. You can't stop God's purpose. God's purpose is greater than you are, and if you are God's child, nothing is going to slow down God's purpose for your life.

August 17

GIVE US GUIDANCE

Teach me to do what You want,
because You are my God.
Let Your good Spirit lead me on level ground.

Psalm 143:10

Lord, help us search Your Word for practical help in our daily lives. Help us to lean on You, and help us to turn to You first. Give us, O Father, Your strength and guidance, and increase our hope.

August 18

CONTROL MY TONGUE

LORD, help me control my tongue;
help me be careful about what I say.
Take away my desire to do evil
or to join others in doing wrong.

Psalm 141:3-4

When we avoid dealing with our mistakes and pretend they don't exist, they usually express themselves in ways that we would not anticipate: anger at someone else, frustration at something else, lack of control.

August 19

SUCH LOVE!

The LORD is pleased with those who respect Him,
with those who trust His love.

Psalm 147:11

$\mathcal{G}$od loves us so much that sometimes He gives us what we need
and not what we ask.

August 20

YOU HAVE BEEN MADE HOLY

"Everyone will respect You, Lord,
and will honor You. Only You are holy.
All the nations will come and worship You,
because the right things
You have done are now made known."

Revelation 15:4

We've been offered so much – when you realize that you have been made holy in God's eyes by the purification of His grace, doesn't it make you want to stay pure? Doesn't this realization make you want to keep from staining God's precious creature that is you?

August 21

A DOGGED FAITH

I will praise the LORD all my life; I will
sing praises to my God as long as I live.

Psalm 146:2

Make your faith an independent dogged faith, firmly planted in God's sacrificed Son on the hill of Calvary. It can never be taken away from you.

August 22

GOD IS IN CONTROL

God's holy people must be patient. They must
obey God's commands and keep their faith in Jesus.

Revelation 14:12

Sometimes storms of life come to teach us that God is in control, that we must lean on Him, and learn to be thankful for the richness of His blessings to us.

August 23

GOD IS WITH YOU

Everything the LORD does is right.
He is loyal to all He has made.

Psalm 145:17

*G*od is with you. God is with you!
The same God that guided His Son
through death and back to life said He
will never leave us or forsake us. He is
right there with you, perhaps even more
in times of crisis than any other time.

August 24

HE PROTECTS ME

Praise the LORD, my Rock, who trains me for war,
who trains me for battle. He protects me like a
strong, walled city, and He loves me. He is my defender
and my Savior, my shield and my protection.

Psalm 144:1-2

*Y*ou may look ahead and see some
crisis coming down the pike and
think, *I'll never be able to handle that*.
You probably couldn't right now, but God
is with you, and He will give you the
strength you need.

August 25

GOD DOESN'T LIE

Hallelujah! Salvation, glory, and power
belong to our God, because His
judgments are true and right.

Revelation 19:1-2

When God makes a promise, He doesn't lie. And His promises are that everything is going to reach fruition someday. Those who have opted to follow God will be with God forever, and everything else will make sense.

August 26

A PURPOSE IN OUR PAIN

We share in the many sufferings of Christ.
In the same way, much comfort
comes to us through Christ.

2 Corinthians 1:5

When we face struggles, we often wonder, *Why?* Years from now, though, we may realize that it was those struggles that taught us something we could not have otherwise learned – that there was a purpose in our pain.

August 27

FORGET THE FAILURES OF THE PAST

"Everything that is hidden will be made clear
and every secret thing will be made known."

Mark 4:22

I wonder if we stay so busy because we're trying to forget yesterday's failures. We do need to forget those failures of the past, but if we never stop to deal with them, the guilt over those old mistakes will hound us and nip at our heels like an ill-behaved puppy.

August 28

OPEN TO THE
COUNSEL OF GOD

Good people will praise His name;
honest people will live in His presence.

Psalm 140:13

In this fast-paced world in which we live, the very thing we need to do is what we often don't do: We need simply to sit still and open our hearts to the counsel of God. Then we will be well prepared for whatever the day brings.

August 29

REJOICE AND BE HAPPY

Hallelujah! Our Lord God, the Almighty, rules.
Let us rejoice and be happy and give God glory.

Revelation 19:6-7

Father, as we set about the task of trying to be Your people, we pray that You'll help us. May we glorify Your name, may we be open-minded, may we be sincere, may we be willing to change and grow. We thank You, Lord, for the privilege of being Your people.

August 30

A GREATER PURPOSE

When people's steps follow the LORD,
God is pleased with their ways.
If they stumble, they will not fall,
because the LORD holds their hand.

Psalm 37:23-24

God's purpose is greater than your
pain, and He has a greater purpose
than your problems. Your crises are not
going to slow down the purpose of God –
have confidence in that.

August 31

FORGET THOSE HURTS!

He can help those who are tempted,
because He Himself suffered and was tempted.

Hebrews 2:18

*R*esentment is when you allow your hurts to turn to hates. When those hates simmer in your heart, they create bitterness and you are the one who suffers. Forget those hurts!

September

September 1

A WORD OF HOPE

The LORD's love never ends; His mercies never stop.
They are new every morning; LORD,
Your loyalty is great. I say to myself,
"The LORD is mine, so I hope in Him."

Lamentations 3:22-24

What do you need most today? Do you need just a word of hope? That's what we all need. And that's what the Word of God does that nothing and no one else can. The Word of God says to us that there is no hopeless situation, no hopeless illness, no hopeless marriage. If there were hopeless situations, then God would have given up long ago.

September 2

THE CONFIDENCE OF FORGIVENESS

LORD, You are kind and forgiving and
have great love for those who call to You.

Psalm 86:5

It's never too late to get a second chance with God. It's never too late! Think about Paul – he had been a murderer and a blasphemer. He had to look into the faces of people whose fathers he had persecuted, whose children he had killed. He could have spent his life looking at yesterday, but he didn't do that. He started life over again in the confidence of His forgiveness.

September 3

HOPE NEVER DISAPPOINTS

And patience produces character, and character produces hope. And this hope will never disappoint us, because God has poured out His love to fill our hearts.

Romans 5:4-5

Here's a checklist of criteria for handling problems: a clear head, a clean heart, a calm soul, and a confident hope.

September 4

THE PROMISE OF SALVATION

Then the LORD will be king over the whole world.
At that time there will be only one LORD,
and His name will be the only name.

Zechariah 14:9

*F*ather, You've given us such a great promise, the promise of salvation. Forgive us, Father, when we sometimes put more hope in the things of this earth than in the incredible promises of Your heaven.

September 5

A VIRTUE THAT BRINGS MUCH JOY

Remember to welcome strangers,
because some who have done this have
welcomed angels without knowing it.

Hebrews 13:2

*H*ere's a suggestion: We should all wear antennas to work, to church, to school — antennas that pick up on people who seem out of place, whose loneliness shows. Why not be the one to approach these folks and extend friendship to them? Maybe you think the last thing you need is another friend. But friendliness — hospitality — is a virtue that brings as much joy to the giver as to the receiver.

September 6

THE GREAT DEPTH
OF YOUR LOVE

But God shows His great love for us in this way:
Christ died for us while we were still sinners.

Romans 5:8

*H*oly Father, You did not have to save us. You didn't have to touch us. Who would have blamed You for turning Your back on the mess that we've made out of this world and allowing us to spin off into oblivion? But when You saw our pain, You came. When You heard our cries, You hastened. Thank You, Father, for the great depth of Your love that never ends.

THE CROSS IS STILL THERE

LORD, all our success is because of
what You have done, so give us peace.

Isaiah 26:12

In the midst of your busyness, the Cross is still there. In the midst of your emptiness, the Cross is still there. The promises of Jesus still stand today. You can claim peace in the midst of a hectic life – not without sacrifice or concentration, but you can do it.

September 8

PART OF AN ETERNAL PLAN

His purpose was that through the church
all the rulers and powers in the heavenly
world will now know God's wisdom.

Ephesians 3:10

The concept of Christ's followers being called the church is part of an eternal purpose. It is something that was dreamed long before the mountains were dreamed up, long before the oceans were conceived, long before the stars were created. We are part of an eternal plan.

BEGIN THE HEALING PROCESS

The God who gives peace be with you all.

Romans 15:33

Are you hurting today? Maybe you need to touch the hem of the Savior's garment. Maybe you need to come home to the only one who has the power to heal your hurting heart. I pray that this will be the day to begin the healing process.

September 10

THIS PRECIOUS COMMODITY

God ... will give you all the seed you need and make
it grow so there will be a great harvest from
your goodness. He will make you rich in every
way so that you can always give freely. And your
giving ... will cause many to give thanks to God.

2 Corinthians 9:10-11

Never before have parents been in such dire straits for this precious commodity we call time. Moms and dads drive an hour to get to work and an hour to get home. By the time they get home, they have to get ready and go to another meeting. There is no way we can be successful parents without giving our children that faithful element of time.

September 11

THE SAME HOLY SPIRIT

We know that we live in God and He lives in us,
because He gave us His Spirit ... Whoever
confesses that Jesus is the Son of God has
God living inside, and that person lives in God.

1 John 4:13, 15

*T*he same Holy Spirit that operates wonderfully inside a person is the exact power that went into a dark tomb where lay the broken and lifeless body of Jesus Christ, and somehow, in a way that no human being can ever explain, breathed life-giving power into that body.

September 12

SEE JESUS IN A NEW WAY

We must not become tired of doing good.
We will receive our harvest of eternal life
at the right time if we do not give up.

Galatians 6:9

Lift up our eyes, Father, that we might see our world as You see it. Hold up our hearts, Father, that we might respond as You respond to the hurts around us. Lord, would You restore the spirit of undying gratitude? May we each day see Jesus in a fresh and new way.

September 13

LAY YOUR CARES AT HIS FEET

Wait for the LORD's help and follow Him.
He will honor you and give you the land,
and you will see the wicked sent away.

Psalm 37:34

*O*nly you can surrender your concerns to the Father. No one else can take those away and give them to God. Only you can cast all your anxieties on the One who cares for you. What better way to start the day than laying your cares at His feet?

September 14

CHILDREN OF GOD

But to all who did accept Him and believe in Him
He gave the right to become children of God.

John 1:12

$\mathcal{F}$ather, You are God and Creator,
but we come to You as children
coming to their father, as children who
would ask their father to hold and comfort
them, hoping to receive words of wisdom.

September 15

MAKE ME STRONG AGAIN

I am sad and tired.
Make me strong again as You have promised.
Psalm 119:28

*P*ain is inevitable, but misery is optional.

September 16

LISTEN TO YOUR OWN HEART

My God, I want to do what You want.
Your teachings are in my heart.

Psalm 40:8

The majority is not always right. If the majority had ruled, the children of Israel never would have left Egypt. They would have voted to stay in bondage. If the majority had ruled, David would have never fought Goliath. His brothers would have voted for him to stay with the sheep. What's the point? You must listen to your own heart.

September 17

KEEP US CLOSE TO YOU

Let everyone who trusts You be happy;
let them sing glad songs forever. Protect those
who love You and who are happy because of You.

Psalm 5:11

Heavenly Father, may Your name be praised. Lord, may we see the joy that is before us? Would You pull back the eternal curtain and give us a glimpse into the everlasting? Would You hear the secret yearnings of our hearts? Will You keep us close to You this day?

September 18

THE COURAGE TO WONDER

They love the LORD's teachings, and they
think about those teachings day and night.
They are strong, like a tree planted by a river.

Psalm 1:2-3

All of us, Father, at one time or another, have wondered if you really are who You say You are. We've looked at the consequences and circumstances of our lives, and wondered why these things happen. We have the courage to wonder, when we read page after page in the Bible sharing the agony of those who sought You. And we find great encouragement from those who found You.

September 19

I WILL TRUST THE LORD

If an army surrounds me, I will not be afraid.
If war breaks out, I will trust the LORD.

Psalm 27:3

here has been a time in the history of this globe when there was not a rain cloud somewhere on the earth. There may be blue skies for us occasionally, but the rain always comes. So, instead of looking for ways to escape problems, look for methods to face them head on.

September 20

THINKING GROUNDED
IN THE WORD

I call to You, God, and You answer me.

Psalm 17:6

Anchor your convictions to the Word of God to help prevent crises from occurring in your life. When facing tough decisions, employ dogged and determined prayer and thinking grounded in the Word.

September 21

HELP US TO SEE JESUS

"I am the Alpha and the Omega,
the Beginning and the End.
I will give free water from the spring of
the water of life to anyone who is thirsty."

Revelation 21:6

*F*ather, we want to see You and know You better. We ask You, Father, to help us see Jesus and to deepen our faith upon seeing Him more clearly.

September 22

GET YOUR BRAIN IN GEAR

"Listen, I am sending you out like sheep among wolves.
So be as clever as snakes and as innocent as doves."

Matthew 10:16

*D*on't retire your brain when you become a follower of Christ. Be a thinker. Jesus told His followers to be shrewd as snakes. The first thing you need to do to solve problems is to get your brain in gear! That may not sound very spiritual, but it's a very practical principle. You need to use your head.

September 23

THE PROMISE OF ETERNAL LIFE

We all share in Christ if we keep till the
end the sure faith we had in the beginning.

Hebrews 3:14

*F*ather, teach us to set our hopes
on heaven, to hold firmly to the
promise of eternal life, so that we can
withstand the struggles and storms of this
world. May Your holy Word be a soothing
medicine to the wounded heart.

September 24

THE LORD PROTECTS MY LIFE

The LORD is my light and the one who saves me.
So why should I fear anyone?
The LORD protects my life. So why should I be afraid?

Psalm 27:1

The Christian in the midst of a crisis doesn't allow everyone's opinion or everyone's feelings to cause him to drift away from what is most important. He sets his anchor deep in the Word and firm in his faith.

September 25

HAVING A SAVIOR IN CHRIST

I pray that the faith you share may make
you understand every blessing we have in Christ.

Philemon 6

*H*aving a Savior in Christ means
that the hopeless have hope,
the dead have life, and the abandoned
have Good News.

THE NATURE OF REPENTANCE

This is what the Lord God, the Holy One of Israel, says:
"If you come back to Me and trust Me,
you will be saved. If you will be calm
and trust Me, you will be strong."

Isaiah 30:15

You look at the love of God and you can't believe He's loved you like He has, and it motivates you to change your life. That is the nature of repentance.

September 27

THE FRESH AIR OF GOD'S FORGIVENESS

Hear their prayers from Your home in heaven.
Forgive and treat each person as he should be
treated because You know what is in a person's heart.
Only You know what is in people's hearts.

2 Chronicles 6:30

Could you use the genuine fresh air of God's forgiveness? Would you love to stand in the approval of God again? How do you do it? By genuinely admitting to God that you've made a mistake, knowing that God loves you more than He hates your mistakes. And knowing that He will forgive those mistakes.

September 28

ANOTHER KINGDOM

I will be glad and rejoice in Your love,
because You saw my suffering; You knew my
troubles. You have not handed me over to
my enemies but have set me in a safe place.

Psalm 31:7–8

Jesus went against the grain. The Messiah was expected to appear like a conquering king heading for the castle. Instead, He spoke of another kingdom. And He spent His time out in the countryside, preaching tenderness, meekness, love, and kindness rather than fire and punishment.

September 29

A DIFFERENCE BETWEEN FAITH AND PRESUMPTION

The LORD shows His true love every day.
At night I have a song, and I pray to my living God.

Psalm 42:8

I believe there's great power in prayer. I believe God heals the wounded, and that He can raise the dead. But I don't believe we tell God what to do and when to do it. You see, there's a difference between faith and presumption. There's a difference between believing He's the Almighty God and demanding He become our divine servant.

September 30

ASK ANY QUESTION

But I will call to God for help, and the LORD
will save me. Morning, noon, and night I am
troubled and upset, but He will listen to me.

Psalm 55:16–17

It's not a sin to doubt. Disbelief
is sin, but questioning – sincerely
seeking – is acceptable to God because
in the presence of God you may ask any
question you want.

October

October 1

THE TRUE TEST OF FAITH

If we are not faithful, He will still be faithful,
because He must be true to who He is.

2 Timothy 2:13

It's not hard to have faith when all of our bills are being paid and our kids are healthy and our marriage is intact. It's not hard to have faith when God gives us everything we want. The true test of faith comes when circumstances are difficult, when our train of hope gets derailed.

October 2

PROCLAIM GOD'S MERCY

Your kingdom is built on what is right and fair.
Love and truth are in all You do.

Psalm 89:14

What are Christians to proclaim? We are to proclaim God's mercy. First and foremost, we must announce to the world that God is a good God. We need to be a source of Good News. And we need to be a source of comfort.

October 3

OUR GOAL

In every way be an example of doing good deeds.
When you teach, do it with honesty and seriousness.

Titus 2:7

If we ever get to the point where our goal is to have people say, "What a wonderful person," we're missing the mark. Instead, our goal is to have people say, "What a wonderful God this person serves." Our task is to have people say, "Tell me about your God," to point people to Him.

MESSENGERS OF GOD'S GRACE

God has chosen you and
made you His holy people.

Colossians 3:12

We should be messengers of God's grace. We should be with the poor what Christ would be with the poor. We should be with the lost what Christ would be with the lost. We should be with the discouraged what Christ would be with the discouraged ... with the sick, the lonely, exactly what Christ would be.

October 5

YOU ARE THE LIGHT

"You are the light that gives light to the world.
A city that is built on a hill cannot be hidden."

Matthew 5:14

When you extend hospitality to others, you're not trying to impress people, you're trying to reflect God to them. You don't have to be rich to be hospitable. A wise friend once told me, "If you won't give people hot dogs when you're poor, you won't give them steaks when you're rich." We shouldn't let our pride get in the way of being hospitable.

October 6

DO YOU HAVE FAITH?

Faith means being sure of the things
we hope for and knowing that something
is real even if we do not see it.

Hebrews 11:1

Do you have faith? If you have faith, then you have what it takes to tackle your problems before they tackle you. If you have that confident hope, then you will know how to handle whatever life brings you.

October 7

OUR QUEST TO REST

"Come to Me, all of you who are tired and
have heavy loads, and I will give you rest."

Matthew 11:28

*P*erhaps the words of the carpenter, promising rest, are so
compelling because of our endless desire
and quest to rest – not just to rest in
the body, but to rest the heart, to find
peace, to finally settle down in a valley
fertile with contentment.

October 8

USE YOUR GOD-GIVEN GIFT

There are different kinds of gifts, but they are all from the same Spirit. There are different ways to serve but the same Lord to serve.

1 Corinthians 12:4-5

You can develop a God-given gift. You may have the gift of encouragement or the gift of teaching or some other gift. What you do with that gift is up to you. You can use your God-given gift to let Christ shine through you.

October 9

DO NOT HOLD BACK YOUR MERCY

LORD, do not hold back Your mercy from me;
let Your love and truth always protect me.

Psalm 40:11

Father, You promised that there would be faith and strength and hope to meet life's problems. Father, give that strength to those whose anxieties have buried their dreams, whose illnesses have hospitalized their hopes, whose burdens are bigger than their shoulders.

October 10

YOKED WITH JESUS

"The path of life is level for those who are
right with God; LORD, You make the way
of life smooth for those people."

Isaiah 26:7

Jesus says, "Take My yoke." He
had made countless yokes as a
carpenter. (A yoke is that instrument
that joins two oxen so they can work
together.) But before we can be yoked
with Jesus, we have to admit we need
Him, don't we? A lot of us are out there
plowing on our own, dragging a yoke
where Jesus is supposed to be.

October 11

THE FIRST STEP

Turn Your face from my sins and wipe out
all my guilt. Create in me a pure heart,
God, and make my spirit right again.

Psalm 51:9-10

The first step toward pardon is the admission of guilt. The first step toward forgiveness is the request for forgiveness.

October 12

THE ONLY PATH TO CONTENTMENT

Do not love the world or
the things in the world.
If you love the world, the love
of the Father is not in you.

1 John 2:15

Do you feel that you've spent your life in endless pursuit of contentment? Do you reach the top of the ladder, and discover you don't want to be there anymore? Do you dream about having the perfect mate, and once you marry, you realize he or she isn't perfect? Contentment is not found in things of this world; the only path to contentment is through Christ.

October 13

JESUS – ANGRY?

Then Jesus criticized the cities where
He did most of His miracles, because the people
did not change their lives and stop sinning.

Matthew 11:20

esus – angry? His fists clenched
and His eyebrows furrowed, His
face getting red, His veins bulging in His
neck, and He's angry. He demands that
the people repent.

October 14

SIMPLY TRUST THE LORD

I was very worried,
but You comforted me and made me happy.

Psalm 94:19

*H*as any good ever come out of any worrying that you've ever done? Worry only compartmentalizes us and makes us unable to do what we set out to do. If you are worried about a problem, what you need to do is simply trust the Lord and do good.

October 15

HIS LAST PUBLIC INVITATION

"Accept My teachings and learn from Me,
because I am gentle and humble in spirit,
and you will find rest for your lives."

Matthew 11:29

Jesus takes a deep breath and turns and looks into the weary faces of the farmers and housewives and businessmen who've come to hear Him speak, and He offers what some consider to be His last public invitation.

October 16

COMBAT IS OPTIONAL

"Do to others what you would want
them to do to you ... Then you will have
a great reward, and you will
be children of the Most High God."

Luke 6:31, 35

*C*onflict is inevitable, but combat is optional. Use your God-given creative energy to solve conflict before it escalates into combat.

October 17

EXTEND YOUR FORGIVENESS

LORD, if You punished people for all their sins,
no one would be left, LORD.
But You forgive us, so You are respected.

Psalm 130:3-4

Extend your forgiveness. If you have been forgiven by God, then there is room for you to forgive another human being. If God has forgiven you, then there is a wellspring of mercy from which you can draw and give to someone else. No one has offended you more than you have already offended God!

October 18

REPAIRING A RELATIONSHIP

You, LORD, give true peace to those who
depend on You, because they trust You.
So, trust the LORD always,
because He is our Rock forever.

Isaiah 26:3-4

In repairing a relationship, it's essential to realize that no friendship is perfect, no marriage is perfect, no person is perfect. With the resolve that you are going to make a relationship work, you can develop peace treaties of love and tolerance and harmony to transform a difficult situation into something beautiful.

October 19

THE SPIRIT HELPS US

The Spirit helps us with our weakness. We do not know how to pray as we should. But the Spirit Himself speaks to God for us, even begs God for us with deep feelings that words cannot explain.

Romans 8:26

*F*ather, we invite You to work in our hearts today. This day would be nothing without Your spirit – convicting, convincing, encouraging, and helping us. We can do nothing on our own and so we ask You for Your help in all we do.

October 20

CARRY MY BURDEN

"I will give rest and strength to
those who are weak and tired."

Jeremiah 31:25

an you say to Jesus, "This burden's too heavy for me. I want You to be my coworker. I want You to carry this burden with me. I cannot do it any longer". He says if you will come to Him, if you'll allow Him to carry that burden with you, His promise is that you will receive rest.

THE ROCK OF
MY PROTECTION

But the LORD is my defender;
my God is the rock of my protection.

Psalm 94:22

If you're facing a problem, perhaps what you need to do is just simply calm down, settle down, and start thinking. Don't try to douse it, don't try to rationalize it. Don't try to escape it. Just think it through, with God's help.

October 22

A COVENANT OF LOVE

You keep Your loving promise and
lead the people You have saved.
With Your strength You will guide
them to Your holy place.

Exodus 15:13

Don't think that God always has goosebumps and happy feelings toward His people. That same God is the God who once wondered if He should have ever made this thing called the human race. But it's the same God who assures us that "you are My people and I will be your God." It's not based on feelings or perfection; it's based on a covenant of love.

THE PRIVILEGE OF SERVING

God began doing a good work in you,
and I am sure He will
continue it until it is finished
when Jesus Christ comes again.

Philippians 1:6

Father, we pray for Your servants who devote their lives to sharing Your Good News throughout the world. We ask Your blessing upon them and we pray that You strengthen them. And Father, lift up our eyes and help us to be aware of people we've never seen, languages we've never heard. We are grateful for the privilege of serving You.

October 24

EXPAND OUR VISION

"There is joy in the presence of the angels of
God when one sinner changes his heart and life."

Luke 15:10

Expand our vision, Father, and help us see the world as You see it. Touch us so that we would grieve over the global sin that causes You to grieve, that we would weep over the world hunger that causes You to weep. Give us the eyes of Christ, that we may see the world as You see it and care for it as You do.

COHEIRS OF ETERNAL SALVATION

Make every effort to give yourself to God
as the kind of person He will approve.
Be a worker who is not ashamed and who
uses the true teaching in the right way.

2 Timothy 2:15

*Y*our home is simply a means to take
you to a greater end – a heavenly
end. Working together as coheirs of eternal
salvation is the foundation for the home.

October 26

LOOK IN YOUR OWN HEART

Light shines on those who do right;
joy belongs to those who are honest.

Psalm 97:11

When we look in our own hearts – honestly, doggedly, prayerfully before God – and realize that perhaps we haven't done as much as we could to make a relationship work, immediately animosity begins to be diluted with tenderness, and understanding begins to surface.

October 27

LOVE YOUR NEIGHBOR

"Love the Lord your God with all your heart,
all your soul, all your strength, and all your mind."
Also, "Love your neighbor as you love yourself."

Luke 10:27

*S*ervanthood is seen when you realize that communication falls to the
speaker and not to the hearer. When
you're communicating with someone, it's
your responsibility to see that the listener
understands. Put yourself in the shoes of
the other person, speak their language,
live their hurts, feel their fears, and help
them.

TO THAT CROSS WE TURN

He is able to protect what He
has trusted me with until that day.

2 Timothy 1:12

*F*ather, in the midst of hectic schedules, we come to You. What was supposed to give us more time seems to take more time to run. What was supposed to free us up seems to imprison us. And, Lord, there are times when the only stability in the world is the Cross of Christ. So to that Cross we turn, praying that You would give us the courage to do only what needs to be done in Your eyes, through Your power.

October 29

GOD DWELLING WITHIN YOU

Know that the LORD is God. He made us, and we belong to Him; we are His people, the sheep He tends.

Psalm 100:3

Dwell on the fact that God lives within you. Think about the power that gives you life. The realization that God is dwelling within you may change the places you want to go and the things you want to do today.

SANCTIFICATION – A LIFELONG PROCESS

All things are worth nothing compared with
the greatness of knowing Christ Jesus my Lord.
Because of Him, I have lost all those things,
and now I know they are worthless trash.

Philippians 3:8

*S*alvation is the process that's done, that's secure, that no one can take away from you. Sanctification is the life-long process of being changed from one degree of glory to the next, growing in Christ, putting away the old, taking on the new.

October 31

A VICTOR IN GOD'S VICTORY

Fight the good fight of faith, grabbing hold of the life that continues forever. You were called to have that life when you confessed the good confession before many witnesses.

1 Timothy 6:12

Do you know why you should feel grateful? You are a part of God's plan, you are touched by God's tenderness, and you are a victor in God's victory. What greater blessing could there be?

November

November 1

AN ACT OF WORSHIP

This is my prayer for you: that your love will grow more and more; that you will have knowledge and understanding with your love ... that you will be filled with the good things produced in your life by Christ to bring glory and praise to God.

Philippians 1:9, 11

When you take food to the poor, that's an act of worship. When you give a word of kindness to someone who needs it, that's an act of worship. When you write someone a letter to encourage them or sit down and open your Bible with someone to teach them, that's an act of worship.

November 2

A REASON TO BE ALIVE

But our homeland is in heaven, and we are waiting
for our Savior, the Lord Jesus Christ, to come
from heaven. By His power to rule all things,
He will change our humble bodies and
make them like His own glorious body.

Philippians 3:20–21

You belong to God's eternal dream. Now you may not feel motivated, you may not feel like you have a reason for living, but you must renew your mind with the immovable fact that you are part of a commissioned people – you have a reason to be alive.

YOUR SINS ARE COVERED

All who believe in Jesus will be forgiven
of their sins through Jesus' name.

Acts 10:43

*T*here are some facts that will never change. One fact is that you are forgiven. If you are in Christ, when He sees you, your sins are covered – He doesn't see them. He sees you better than you see yourself. And that is a glorious fact of your life.

November 4

MORE LIKE JESUS

LORD, show Your love to us
as we put our hope in You.

Psalm 33:22

God, give us strength as we try to be more like Jesus in our homes. We ask You to keep the evil one away from us; keep us close. Let our homes be testimonies of Your love for us, that when people see our homes, they would see how You have loved the world.

MAKE AN ETERNAL DIFFERENCE

Also pray for us that God will give us an opportunity
to tell people His message. Pray that we can preach
the secret that God has made known about Christ.

Colossians 4:3

We are here on earth to be God's people. We are here to show others the same God who came to be a friend to the earth — that's our task. Maybe today you will meet someone who really needs a friend — and you can fill that need. Maybe you can make an eternal difference in that person's life, just because you choose to be friendly today.

November 6

FORGIVE AND LET GO

Those who love Your teachings will find true peace,
and nothing will defeat them.

Psalm 119:165

The God who is willing to forgive you has already forgiven you much more than you could ever forgive anyone else. The best thing you can do to bring peace to your life is to forgive the mistakes of others. I'm not saying to justify their mistakes; I'm saying forgive them and let go.

November 7

POWERFUL INDWELLING

But LORD, You are our father. We are like clay,
and You are the potter; Your hands made us all.

Isaiah 64:8

$\mathcal{F}$ather, we invite Your assistance and guidance and powerful indwelling, because we do not have the strength to be transformed into Your likeness and not be conformed to this world. May we understand more of what it means to say, "It is well with my soul."

PURSUIT OF THINGS

"It is worthless to have the
whole world if they lose their souls.
They could never pay enough
to buy back their souls."

Matthew 16:26

Being busy is not a sin. Jesus was busy. Paul was busy. Peter was busy. Nothing of significance is achieved without effort and hard work and weariness. That, in and of itself, is not a sin. But being busy in an endless pursuit of *things* that leave us empty and hollow and broken inside — that cannot be pleasing to God.

November 9

THAT SAME POWER

The LORD made the earth by His power.
He used His wisdom to build the world and
His understanding to stretch out the skies.

Jeremiah 51:15

*T*he power that lives in God's children is the same power that was
present at the Creation, calling into being
this existence that we call the world. That
same power was present, inspiring David,
inspiring the prophets. That same power
is alive today to convince you, convict
you, equip you, and encourage you.

OUR BODIES BECOME TEMPLES

Dear friends, we have these promises from God,
so we should make ourselves pure — free from
anything that makes body or soul unclean.
We should try to become holy in the
way we live, because we respect God.

2 Corinthians 7:1

*G*od has chosen to dwell in us, and our bodies become much more than carcasses carrying around flesh and bone. Our bodies become temples in which God has chosen to dwell.

November 11

SETTING US FREE

LORD, You bless those who do what is right;
You protect them like a soldier's shield.

Psalm 5:12

Thank You, Father, for setting us
free. May we be spurred on by
Your love to do great works, yet never
substituting those works for Your great
grace. May we always hear Your voice.
Keep us free from our own legalism, our
own systems. Keep us amazed and mes-
merized by what You have done for us.

November 12

HEAL THEIR WOUNDS

The LORD gives strength to His people;
the LORD blesses His people with peace.

Psalm 29:11

Father, I would pray a special prayer for those who have gone through divorce. Will You give them peace? Will You hold them in the palm of Your hand and heal their wounds as only You can?

SEE HIS MERCY

The LORD is kind and shows mercy.
He does not become angry quickly but is full of love.

Psalm 145:8

The first step in finding your place in God's plan is to see His mercy – instead of looking inside yourself, look up to Him and reflect upon and understand His mercy. How great is the call of God!

ALL-WEEK-LONG WORSHIP

Come into His city with songs of thanksgiving
and into His courtyards with songs of praise.
Thank Him and praise His name.

Psalm 100:4

Our biblical act of worship is not what we do on Sunday mornings in coats and ties, but our act of worship is a lifelong, seven-days-a-week process of placing ourselves upon an altar of sacrifice. Worship is living the principles of Christ in everything we do. You're worshiping God by what you do all week long.

November 15

GRACE

Because He was full of grace and truth,
from Him we all received one gift after another.

John 1:16

Grace is a pleasant surprise. Grace is a kind gesture. Grace is something you did not expect. It is something you certainly could never earn. But grace is something you'd never turn down.

November 16

SPEAK UP AND HELP THE HOPELESS

Speak up for those who cannot speak for themselves;
defend the rights of all those who have nothing.
Speak up and judge fairly, and defend
the rights of the poor and the needy.

Proverbs 31:8-9

*J*esus demonstrated His tenderness by helping those people forgotten by society: He helped the deaf, He helped the lepers, He helped the blind, He helped the crippled. This was how He proved that He was the Messiah: He had a different way of looking at people. He helped those who had no hope.

November 17

HARDENED HEARTS

Happy is the person whose sins are forgiven,
whose wrongs are pardoned. Happy is
the person whom the LORD does not consider
guilty and in whom there is nothing false.

Psalm 32:1-2

*F*ather, have mercy on our hard-
ened hearts. Forgive us for being
witnesses of Your majesty and yet living
like You did not exist. Teach us the
meaning of repentance, Father.

November 18

HARMONY

You have chosen to bless my family.
Let it continue before You always. LORD, You have
blessed my family, so it will always be blessed.

1 Chronicles 17:27

God's goal for your home is harmony. That means a family of individuals singing different notes, but with the same score of music, with the same goal.

November 19

I'M YOURS

"So I tell you, ask, and God will give to you.
Search, and you will find.
Knock, and the door will open for you."

Luke 11:9

Surrendering our lives to Christ means going to Him and saying, "I'm Yours; use me however You want to." Once you've done this, you can begin to seek His will for your life.

November 20

FOCUSING ON THE FATHER

You do great and wonderful things, Lord God Almighty.
Everything the Lord does is right and true,
King of the nations.

Revelation 15:3

In the midst of a busy life on the freeway of humanity, it seems that the faster we go, the emptier we become. When we're always in a hurry trying to get ahead, never taking time to pause and reflect, we sacrifice a lot to stay on top. Sometimes it takes hard decisions to bring our lives under control and realign our priorities, focusing on the Father and letting everything else take a backseat.

November 21

HEAR MY PRAYER

Answer me when I pray to You, my God who does what is right. Make things easier for me when I am in trouble. Have mercy on me and hear my prayer.

Psalm 4:1

God knows that we with our limited vision don't even know that for which we should pray. And we are praying for things right now that God knows would not be best for us. When we entrust our requests to Him, we trust Him to honor our prayers with holy judgment.

November 22

UNQUENCHABLE LOVE

The LORD doesn't become angry quickly,
but He has great love.
He forgives sin and law breaking.

Numbers 14:18

No matter what you do, no matter how far you fall, no matter how ugly you become, God has a relentless, undying, unfathomable, unquenchable love from which you cannot be separated. Ever!

IF YOU BELIEVE

"If you believe, you will get anything
you ask for in prayer."

Matthew 21:22

*P*arents, don't give up. It's not too
late for the child who has brought
only tears. Think of Jesus' parents; the
mother who had to watch her Son crucified
saw her Son raised from the dead. Though
you may go to the grave wondering if your
prayers will ever be answered, don't stop
praying. God blesses faithfulness.

THINGS THAT NEVER SATISFY

The person with understanding
is always looking for wisdom,
but the mind of a fool wanders everywhere.

Proverbs 17:24

One source of man's weariness is the pursuit of things that can never satisfy, but which one of us has not been caught up in that pursuit at some time in our lives? Our passions, possessions, and pride – these are all *dead* things. When you try to get life out of dead things, the result is only weariness and dissatisfaction.

November 25

FAITH AND FAMILY

LORD, Your love reaches to
the heavens, Your loyalty to the skies.

Psalm 36:5

As an air force general addressed
five or six hundred military per-
sonnel at his retirement party, he said
that the priorities of his life were first, his
faith and second, his family. "As I en-
tered the military, I knew that someday I
would leave it. If I made the military my
whole life, what would happen when this
day came? But with my life centered on
faith and family, I still have everything!"

THE TRUE VOICE OF JESUS CHRIST

Depend on the LORD and His strength;
always go to Him for help.

1 Chronicles 16:11

*F*ather, help us to say no to the world and yes to You. Help us to hear the true voice of Jesus Christ amid the voices of pressure and success and power. We don't really know how, unless You come and help us.

THE GIFTS YOU HAVE

God never changes His mind about the
people He calls and the things He gives them.

Romans 11:29

I look at some gifted people – some God-given gifted people – and oftentimes I wish I could do what they do. But God doesn't want us to feel guilty. Use the gifts you have, because God never calls us to do more than that for which He has equipped us.

EXAMINE YOUR OWN HEART

May the patience and encouragement that
come from God allow you to live in harmony with
each other the way Christ Jesus wants.

Romans 15:5

When you have a relationship in need of repair, the first key to improvement is to examine your own heart. Look at your own heart – remember who you are and who God called you to be. Did the Father call you to be angry? To be bitter? Or did He call you to be loving and forgiving?

November 29

GOD'S POWER

Your love is wonderful. By Your power You save
those who trust You from their enemies.
Protect me as You would protect Your own eye.
Hide me under the shadow of Your wings.

Psalm 17:7-8

$\mathcal{S}$imply because you can't put your
hands around something doesn't
mean it's not there. In fact, those things
that are most precious to us are the
things that are invisible, aren't they?
Love, tenderness, happiness, air, feelings, emotions – those things we cannot
touch, but they are very real. And so it is
with God's power: It may not be touch-
able, but it's real and it's obtainable.

November 30

REMAIN TRUE

Now we hope for the blessings God
has for His children. These blessings, which
cannot be destroyed or be spoiled or
lose their beauty, are kept in heaven for you.

1 Peter 1:4

It's not easy to hear the voice of God when popular opinion tells you it's okay to be immoral, or when your friends cheat on their income tax. But if you remain true to what you know to be right and godly, God says you will be blessed.

December

December 1

SET FREE BY YOUR GRACE

"My grace is enough for you. When you are weak,
My power is made perfect in you."

2 Corinthians 12:9

*F*ather, will You please help us to forgive others? Help us to forgive the one who has hurt us the most. And help us to forgive ourselves – even as You have forgiven us – that we might not live burdened and shackled by yesterday's failures, but that we might live set free by Your grace.

December 2

ALL BASED ON LOVE

The Son of God has come and has given us
understanding so that we can know the True One.
And our lives are in the True One and in His Son,
Jesus Christ. He is the true God and the eternal life.

1 John 5:20

*F*ather, we look at Your plan and
it's all based on love, not on our
performance, and we pray that You'd
help us to understand that. To be capti-
vated by Your love. To be overwhelmed
by Your grace. To come home to You
in that beautiful path that You've already
carved out for us.

December 3

LIVE IN PEACE

Live in peace with each other.
1 Thessalonians 5:13

*T*hat "peace that passes understanding" cannot be obtained if we
sacrifice valuable relationships at the expense of fleeting gratifications.

December 4

CONCENTRATE ON THE NECESSARY

My child, listen and accept what I say.
Then you will have a long life. I am guiding you
in the way of wisdom, and I am leading you
on the right path. Nothing will hold you back;
you will not be overwhelmed.

Proverbs 4:10-12

If you want to bring under control a fast-paced lifestyle, you must eliminate the unnecessary; if you want to be where God wants you to be, you must concentrate on the necessary.

December 5

FULL OF DISCIPLINE

The love of money causes all kinds of evil.
1 Timothy 6:10

*H*ere's something that's important to remember: Forget tomorrow's material pleasures because giving in to them can spoil your long-term devotion to your family with the burden of needless debt. You need to be dogged, determined, and full of discipline to avoid this trap.

December 6

THAT KIND OF FRIEND

A friend loves you all the time,
and a brother helps in time of trouble.

Proverbs 17:17

A good lesson on the faithfulness of a friend, is in the story of the paralytic whose friends took him to be healed by Jesus. When they saw crowds of people hanging outside the windows and door, it would have been easy for those friends to turn back. Instead, they cut a hole in the roof and lowered their sick friend down to Jesus. What loyalty of friendship! Are you that kind of friend?

December 7

REWARD FOR FAITHFULNESS

Dear friends, now we are children of God,
and we have not yet been shown what
we will be in the future. But we know that
when Christ comes again, we will be like Him,
because we will see Him as He really is.

1 John 3:2

*A*ny difficulties we face in life are short-lived; all rewards are eternal. A divine inheritance will be our reward for faithfulness to our heavenly Father. Our faithfulness to the Father is something we should renew daily – a priority for beginning our day.

December 8

HEAR OUR QUESTIONS

Lord, I know that our lives don't really belong to us.
We can't control our own lives.
Lord, correct me, but be fair.

Jeremiah 10:23-24

We pray, O Father, that in the hours when we find ourselves in the dungeons of doubt, that You would hear our questions. Forgive us for demanding that You answer our questions like we want them to be answered. Forgive us for having certain expectations that we think You should meet.

December 9

YOUR SPIRITUAL GUIDE

This God is our God forever and ever.
He will guide us from now on.

Psalm 48:14

*Y*ou don't need anybody to intervene between you and God. The Scriptures are available to every person, and the gospel is simple; we can understand it. You need only God to be your spiritual guide.

December 10

DESTINATION: HEAVEN

Jesus, the One who says these things are true, says,
"Yes, I am coming soon." Amen. Come, Lord Jesus!

Revelation 22:20

*G*ood will triumph. God will win. The fate of our enemy, Satan, is sealed. With God as our guide, our destination is heaven. Hallelujah!

December 11

SET FREE

Love the LORD your God with all your heart,
all your soul, all your mind, and all your strength.

Mark 12:30

God wants to emancipate His people; He wants to set them free. He wants His people to be not slaves but sons. He wants them governed not by law but by love.

December 12

TOTALLY DEPENDENT ON HIM

It does not belong to us, LORD.
The glory belongs to You
because of Your love and loyalty.

Psalm 115:1

I believe that many of us go through life sucking on pacifiers. Oh, we don't see them because they're in our bank. Or they're parked in our garage. Or we live in them. Jesus wants us to be totally dependent on Him so that we might fortify our faith.

December 13

THE RIGHT PERSPECTIVE

God, I will thank You forever for what
You have done. With those who worship You,
I will trust You because You are good.

Psalm 52:9

Gratitude comes from having the right
perspective. It's being able to look
at what you have and being thankful for
that, rather than longing for what you
don't have.

WHEN THE GOING GETS TOUGH

The LORD God is like a sun and shield; the LORD gives us kindness and honor. He does not hold back anything good from those whose lives are innocent.

Psalm 84:11

If God has been with you this far, He's not going to leave you when you're in troubled times. If your faith has brought you this far, don't throw your faith out when the going gets tough.

December 15

DIFFERENT FROM US?

God looked down from heaven on
all people to see if anyone was wise,
if anyone was looking to God for help.

Psalm 53:2

In one of the greatest testimonies to the authenticity of Scripture, the Word of God doesn't avoid showing the weaknesses of man; it doesn't cover up the unpleasant, it doesn't hide the dents in the armor. In an honest look at humanity, we read that Abraham doubted, that Moses lost his temper, that Peter denied his Lord. These chosen men of God – were they so different from us?

December 16

HONEST QUESTIONS

"Remember that I commanded you to be strong and brave. Don't be afraid, because the Lord your God will be with you everywhere you go."

Joshua 1:9

God never turns His back on those who ask honest questions. He never did in the Old Testament; He never did in the New Testament. So if you are asking honest questions of God, He will not turn away from you.

December 17

OPENING OUR HEARTS

LORD, every morning You hear my voice.
Every morning, I tell You what I need,
and I wait for Your answer.

Psalm 5:3

*F*ather, we confess that sometimes prayer isn't very easy. We don't see You, and we don't see You hearing our words, but we have so many experiences in our own lives where prayers have been answered by faith that we continue coming before You, opening our hearts to You through prayer.

December 18

YOUR REPENTANT HEART

Without faith no one can please God. Anyone who comes to God must believe that He is real and that He rewards those who truly want to find Him.

Hebrews 11:6

Have you ever avoided the embrace of God in order to receive the acceptance of your peers? Have you, then, experienced the genuine turning of your repentant heart back to the Father and felt His consuming acceptance?

December 19

SMALL TROUBLES

We have small troubles for a while now,
but they are helping us gain an eternal glory
that is much greater than the troubles.

2 Corinthians 4:17

*F*ather, thank You, for carrying us when we struggle. We're grateful that You don't turn Your back when we're in trouble. Help us not to minimize our struggles, and yet at the same time, help us recognize that any struggle we have is small in comparison to the great God we serve.

December 20

THE RIGHT THING TO DO

Only the LORD gives wisdom; He gives knowledge
and understanding ... Then you will
understand what is honest and fair and
what is the good and right thing to do.

Proverbs 2:6, 9

*N*ever let your decisions be made
on the basis of the blowings of
the winds of opinions and popularity.

December 21

THAT CANDLE OF HOPE

I find rest in God;
only He gives me hope.

Psalm 62:5

*I*f hope dies, we begin to die, don't we? As long as we can keep that candle of hope lit, as long as we can keep that spark of possibility afire, then we can stay strong.

December 22

A MESSAGE OF LIFE

Praise be to the God and Father of our
LORD Jesus Christ. In God's great mercy He has
caused us to be born again into a living hope,
because Jesus Christ rose from the dead.

1 Peter 1:3

The life of Jesus Christ is a message
of hope, a message of mercy, a
message of life in a dark world.

December 23

FOR THE SAKE OF THIS SPECIAL CHILD

"The Lord has blessed you and is with you ...
Don't be afraid, Mary; God has shown you His grace."

Luke 1:28, 30

*M*aybe God chose Mary because He knew she would be the one to fortify herself, to be embroiled in inner turmoil for the sake of this special child. It wasn't easy raising the Son of God. And Mary was the one who would sit at His bedside at night and look at this One who didn't look like a king and wonder, *What am I supposed to do?*

December 24

THE PATTERN FOR PEACE

Agree with each other, and live in peace.
Then the God of love and peace will be with you.

2 Corinthians 13:11

Those who call themselves followers of God need to deal with the issue of peace seriously: There will be peace on earth only when there is peace between man and God. After all, the pattern for peace comes from heaven itself – in Jesus, who reconciled earth to God through the Cross.

December 25

A STAR IN THE DARKNESS

Christ had no sin, but God made Him become sin
so that in Christ we could become right with God.

2 Corinthians 5:21

A wise man saw a star in the east and exclaimed to his companions, "There's a big star – there's a beautiful star in the darkness!" How symbolic for what Jesus was – he was a star in the midst of darkness. For though he was in the midst of sinful people, he did not engage in their sins, and though he was offered a taste of sin, he never took it.

December 26

A PERSONAL INVITATION

LORD, tell me Your ways. Show me how to live.
Guide me in Your truth, and teach me,
my God, my Savior. I trust You all day long.

Psalm 25:4–5

*W*hen Jesus says, "Come to Me," He doesn't say come to religion, come to a system, or come to a certain doctrine. This is a very personal invitation to a God, an invitation to a Savior.

December 27

MISTAKES TURNED INTO OPPORTUNITIES

I can do all things through Christ,
because He gives me strength.

Philippians 4:13

God can take our mistakes and turn them into opportunities. He's shown us, over and over, through the lives of people like David, Paul, Peter. He can do the same for us.

December 28

WHERE TO FIND REST

I said to myself, "Relax, because
the LORD takes care of you."

Psalm 116:7

Do you know where to find rest? Where you find a clean con-science? Where you find the ability to sleep at night and live with yourself? By living in the pleasure of the Father who made you.

December 29

SAFE PASSAGE

Those who go to God Most High for
safety will be protected by the Almighty.
I will say to the LORD,
"You are my place of safety and protection.
You are my God and I trust You."

Psalm 91:1-2

*L*isten to the counsel of God,
re-establish your roots, and pray.
This is the only way to achieve safe
passage through a crisis in your life.

December 30

WE'RE NOT ALONE

The LORD is my strength and shield.
I trust Him, and He helps me.

Psalm 28:7

God did not leave you as an orphan. He says He will be with you always. All of us could use some more strength – who isn't trying to tackle an attitude or put away a bad habit or overcome guilt? We can't see the power, but it's real – we're not alone.

December 31

THE SPECIAL GIFT OF GRACE

Christ gave each one of us the special gift of grace,
showing how generous He is.

Ephesians 4:7

The more we are loved by God, the more we are going to love. The more we are forgiven, the more we're willing to forgive. The more we're treated with patience, the more we are willing to treat others with patience. These are all extensions of that gift of grace.